When God Commanded:

"Build That Wall!"

A Study in the Book of Nehemiah

Plus, The Evil Within

By

Effie Darlene Barba

TABLE OF CONTENTS

THE EVIL WITHIN

Introduction

History has a way of repeating itself; particularly, when we allow ourselves to forget the truths we should have learned along the way. Such was the case with the nation of Israel, who repeatedly forgot the grace and mercy God showered upon them when they sought Him and the chastisement whenever they turned away. Instead of remembering God's Grace as the source of their prosperity; they would become so content with the blessings of prosperity that they would forget the very God who had provided the prosperity. In other words, they would begin to worship the gifts rather than the Giver of the gifts.

Therefore, periods of prosperity led them into gleeful forgetfulness. Once more, they would begin to forsake the laws God had given them to keep them safe. Instead, their eyes, then their hearts; would turn to self-gratification with a sense of invincibility. Thereby, forsaking the truth; they enthusiastically allowed others into their fold who did not share their ideals. Instead of these immigrants adopting the faith of Israel; the nation allowed the mingling of ideologies. Ultimately, the nation began to worship idols; forsaking their own faith. This did not happen once or twice; but, repetitively. Over and over again, this was the story of their history. They cried to God. He in mercy saved them and gave them prosperity and refuge again. They forsook God; and trials came, God would warn them of impending judgement. The people ignored Him, judgement came. Then, they cried for help and God saved them.

Were it not for Grace and God's abiding faithfulness to His covenant; all would have been utterly lost. Yet, God's gracious hand would reach out to save the nation for the few, the remnant of faithful would be brought forth once more into a place of freedom. Securely protected by God's promise to save all those who would seek Him, He would reach forth to restore His people. These were the chosen race from whom the Messiah would be born. The Birth, Death, and Resurrection of Jesus Christ would come through the lineage of Abraham and King David; as God had promised.

Yet, for the protection of those faithful followers; there were moments when the entire nation faced judgment. For were God to have allowed the evil ideologies to abide; all would have been lost. Evil ideologies always grow like a cancer that invades every aspect until all of truth and righteousness die. The battle against such evil ideologies has been raging since Adam chose to willingly disobey God; because, he desired to be god of his own destiny. All too often, the same choice you or I wish to make. The choice that nations tend to make as well; turning their back on the only true hope of peace, joy, and truth which is found only in a relationship with God.

Having been originally formed by God's covenant with Abraham, Israel has stood as a nation; throughout the years, despite their moments of captivity and failure. We can as a nation, learn much from their heritage; both from their mistakes, as well as, their victories.

During one of their greatest periods of prestige and power under King Solomon, the nation of Israel was admired by all of the nations around them. As an act of benevolence and a show of great tolerance, believing himself invincible; King Solomon married women from many nations. This was a way of sealing diplomatic ties with all their surrounding nations.

However, the women and families brought into the nation did not integrate; instead, they spoke their own language, taught the children their customs, and worshipped pagan gods. They had no desire to learn of the one true God whom the nation of Israel worshipped.

Strife grew within the nation and Solomon to appease his wives; began to worship the Pagan gods as well. For many years, I mourned because of Solomon's fate. Often, I searched scripture in hopes to discover a ray of hope for this man who began with such faith and ended in sorrow; then, finally one day I discovered these verses.

When David had wanted to build the temple for God, he was told no. He was told that it would be Solomon who would build the temple. And God promised *"Behold a son shall be born to you, who shall be a man of rest; and I will give him rest from all his enemies all around. His name shall be Solomon, for I will give peace and quietness to Israel in his days. He shall build a house for My name, and he shall be My son, and I will be his father; and I will establish the throne of his kingdom over Israel forever"* (I Chronicles 22:9-10, NKJV).

Furthermore, God had promised David,

> *"And when thy days be fulfilled, and thou shalt sleep with thy fathers, I will set up thy seed after thee, which shall proceed out of thy bowels, and I will establish his kingdom. He shall build a house for my name, and I will stablish the throne of his kingdom for ever. I will be his father, and he shall be my son. If he commit iniquity, I will chasten him with the rod of men, and with the stripes of the children of men: but my mercy shall not depart away from him (2 Samuel 7:12-15, NKJV).*

So, there it was. God's Grace and God's promise to David: God would not depart from Solomon. Oh, the sweetness of knowing we are secure in Him; because, He is faithful to keep His covenant. One day I will meet Solomon in heaven; because, God was faithful and never departed from Him, even though King Solomon had turned to idol worship for a time at the end of his days.

As you see, I got side tracked for a moment to expound upon the Grace of God; even, in the Old Testament. For it has always been Grace and grace alone that has reached out to mankind throughout the ages; since, the moment Adam and Eve chose the creation over the creator.

But can we blame them without pointing a thumb at our own heart as well? I daresay, no; but, standing each one of us as deserving of condemnation;

how humbled we are that God considers us, to offer us His Grace by paying the penalty for our own sins.

But, why would a loving, omnipotent God have allowed evil at all? I promise you that I will address that before the end of this book within the second section of the book, titled "The Evil Within". For now, I will say; true love demands, the beloved be given free will to choose. Unless the beloved can see clearly, honestly what they are choosing; how, can they know they are loved? How can they experience the depth of joy or even understand the Glory of God's Grace; were it not for being given the chance to see clearly and to choose His love. But, there is much more than can fit into this introduction; so, I will address that further before the book ends.

This book will be divided into two parts. The first is a study in the book of Nehemiah; and its importance in the history of Israel as a nation. Then, in part two, "The Evil Within", I will take a closer look at what has happened over the past century in the United States that has led us to where we are today.

There is a closer correlation than we would like to admit to what occurred in Israel during the time leading up to Nehemiah and to what we face as a nation today.

Finally, we will conclude with comparisons in how God restored the nation of Israel; and what we as a nation need to do, if we hope to move forward as a nation.

CHAPTER ONE:

A BROKEN WALL AND DESPAIR

The wall surrounding Jerusalem had been laid in rumbles, burned by the enemies who had ravaged their city. Why was the broken wall a symbol of despair; even to those who now were returning to their land? Much of that I dealt with in a previous study of Nahum, Habakkuk and Zephaniah entitled *When Injustice and Violence Reign*; but, we must review some of the history here, so that you may understand the significance of Nehemiah.

The story of Israel had always been strewn with moments of faith, followed by self-exaltation of the people, a subsequent denial of God's greatness, rebellion of the people, idolatrous living, chastisement,

1

crying out to God with desperation, repentance, and God's Grace reaching out to restore them as a nation.

Finally, with David as King, they followed God; and it would appear all would be well. Under King Solomon, they grew in power, wealth and prestige throughout the world. At their peak, they became lax once more. This time, many new ideologies entered the prosperous nation.

Tolerance, benevolence and a sense of invincibility caused them to allow in many who did not hold their same ideals, regarding God nor the nation of Israel. Even Solomon's heart was turned by these diplomatic marriages; *"For it was so, when Solomon was old, that his wives turned his heart after other gods; and his heart was not loyal to the Lord his God, as was the heart of his father* David (1 Kings 11:3-5, NKJV).

The problem grew with the next generation; because, they had already been indoctrinated with these new ideals and did not hold fast to the truths of their history, nor their faith in God. This led to a division between the ten tribes of the Jewish nation of the North from the other two tribes in the South. The ten tribes making up the Northern Kingdom fell to the Assyrians first. Ignoring the warnings of God, the Southern Kingdom fell to the Babylonian King Nebuchadnezzar after he overthrew the Assyrians.

As a divided nation, their strength to withstand evil had been diminished

As a divided nation, their strength to withstand evil had been diminished; leading to their captivity by the Babylonians. Just as God promised, after seventy years of exile; the remnant of faithful believers began to return to Jerusalem to rebuild. Under Zerubbabel, a descendent of David; the first group returned and built the temple. Then Ezra, a priest, lead the second group. Years later, God called a layman, Nehemiah, to "build that wall."

Why was a wall needed? According to the report Nehemiah received, the remnant in Jerusalem was shamed. A city with broken walls revealed a defeated people. The Jews who had returned to their homeland were both in unsafe conditions and humiliated at living in a destroyed city.... rebuilding the walls showed that God was with His people.[1]

Nehemiah 6:16 refers to this fact, after the wall was completed. *"And it came to pass, that when all our*

---

[1] "Why Was It Important to Rebuild the Walls of Jerusalem?", Got Questions Ministries, accessed November 6, 2017, https://www.gotquestions.org/rebuild-walls-Jerusalem.html.

enemies heard thereof, and all the heathen that were about us saw these things, they were much cast down in their own eyes: for they perceived that this work was wrought of our God." The wall symbolized God's hand of protection for the people. Every day when the people walked in the streets prior to its restoration, the broken wall was a source of despair. It was a constant reminder of their vulnerability as a nation. Shame, sorrow, despair, and fear plagued these who had returned; because, they saw the ravaged wall and felt helpless. The task appeared too great and those opposing the wall too many. They had no way to protect themselves from those who wanted to cause them harm. Evil ideologies surrounded their children and they could know no real rest or peace; yet, they felt too feeble to do anything. They needed a leader.

A BROKEN WALL

When Nebuchadnezzar took Judah captive, he destroyed the temple and destroyed the wall.

And the LORD God of their fathers sent to them by his messengers, rising up betimes, and sending; because he had compassion on his people, and on his dwelling place: But they mocked the messengers of God, and despised his words, and misused his prophets, until the wrath of the LORD arose against his people, till there was no remedy.

Therefore, he brought upon them the king of the Chaldees, who slew their young men with the sword in the house of their sanctuary, and had no compassion upon young man or maiden, old man, or him that stooped for age: he gave them all into his hand.

And all the vessels of the house of God,

great and small, and the treasures of the

house of the LORD, and the treasures of

the king, and of his princes; all these he

brought to Babylon.

And they burnt the house of God,

and brake down the wall of Jerusalem,

and burnt all the palaces thereof with

fire, and destroyed all the goodly vessels

thereof (2 Chronicles 36: 15-19).

God had pleaded with His people. He knew that continuing down the path of sin and idolatrous living would destroy any hope of happiness. Happiness could only be found in God, their creator who knew exactly what their hearts needed to be satisfied. But alas, they did not heed His warnings. In order, to save the few that were faithful; judgment would have to come upon them all. The righteous would suffer, alongside the unrighteous; that the nation could be cleansed.

The righteous would suffer, alongside the unrighteous; that the nation could be cleansed.

God knew there was no other way to save the nation; except to allow their destruction. Only then, would they follow Him. Indeed, they had undergone a magnificent revival under King Josiah; only to forget again and turn to idolatrous worship after his death.

Perhaps, too often during our moments of great faith, peace and joy in the Lord; we, become complacent. Forgetting to read our Bibles or to pray. We tend to forget that it was our prayer and communion with Him that lead to our peace and joy.

We, are so often; **just like that** in our Christian walk. But for us as was the case of the nation of Israel, there is hope; because, chastisement will come to lead us back to close fellowship with Him, the only true source of our joy and peace.

However, there is another truth we must remember. Those who have heard the truth of the gospel message and have turned away, there is only left judgment, if they do not awaken to the truth; turn their eyes to seek God, and ask Him into their hearts. God's judgment may reign down upon all, the just and the unjust; however, those who know Him as Lord, will in the times of captivity hold fast to His promises, as did Daniel and his friends. They remained filled with hope, faith, strength, and a companionship of God's joy in their hearts. Let's look at such a scripture in Hebrews which tells us of God's judgment upon all those who have heard the gospel message, and refused it.

FEARFUL AWAITING OF JUDGMENT

For if we sin willfully after that we have received the knowledge of the truth, there remaineth no more sacrifice for sins, But a certain fearful looking for of judgment and fiery indignation, which shall devour the adversaries (Hebrews 10: 26-27).

This is not saying those who have accepted Christ as their Lord and Savior, can lose their salvation. It is saying, those who have heard the truth and reject it; have no hope.

For the nation of Israel, they awaited the Messiah. However, the majority were seeking worldly pleasures; doing whatever they wanted. Having been given the truth, they rejected it. Now judgment would come. Unfortunately, the righteous would also suffer; however, theirs would be the sweet redemption one day. God promised that, they believed it. In this world, Christians will suffer or even die for the name of Christ. But one day, He will return for His own.

GOD CALLED NEHEMIAH,

"BUILD THAT WALL!"

Well back to the story at hand. The first group of faithful returned to Jerusalem as soon as they heard the decree of Cyrus. Of the millions scattered, only a few returned. Many chose to stay where they were in new lands among their former captors. They had grown comfortable in their new lifestyle. "The people who returned to the land of promise were publicly acknowledging that they believed God would reestablish the nation and usher in a time of kingdom blessing"[2] (Martin 2004)

---

[2] John A. Martin, "Ezra", *The Bible Knowledge Commentary:* John Walvoord and Roy Zuck, eds., (Colorado Springs: CO: Victor, 2004), 651

Those who returned still faced many challenges. Many enemies still entered their city. Their temple was always at risk of being attacked. Yet, as long as the wall lay in shambles, it was a reminder of their vulnerability as a nation. Most lived in despair.

Attacked from every side by the opposition; they desperately needed the wall to symbolize who they were as a nation. They needed the wall to stand strong as a symbol that God was their protector. Beyond that, they knew that without the wall, they were open to being victimized by radical ideologies and people who hated all they stood for.

That is, they remained motionless in their feelings of defeat; until God Commanded Nehemiah to "build that wall!".

CONCLUDING THOUGHTS FOR YOU AND ME

What could all this possibly mean for us? Everything! We must turn our eyes to the only one who can provide hope amid the turmoil and evil we see around us. Just as God preserved and re-established His people in the Old Testament, He will today. If only we would trust Him.

Oh, yes; we may face continued trials on this journey. However, we can trust He who promised to provide us His best. He is the treasure we seek. Take time to read your Bible and sit alone with God. If you do not know Him, I urge you to consider Him today.

Effie Darlene Barba

CHAPTER 2:

When God Breaks Your Heart, What Then?

Nehemiah was called by God to build the wall; but, why Nehemiah? What characteristics made Nehemiah the perfect man for the task? Well, at the beginning of the story; Nehemiah was the cupbearer to King Artaxerxes. He was among those who were very content to stay behind comfortable in the prestigious job he had.

As the book opens, something was about to shake up his contentment. Indeed, he would be suddenly broken hearted. That broken-hearted state, would be the catalyst to transforming this layman into a powerful man of God who would then hear God's call, answer God's call and see the task through to completion.

He would rebuild the wall, and as governor would guide the people back into a place of political, social, and economic stability; while, drawing them back to faith in God. The faithful followers of God would no longer remain the target of ridicule and abuse.

Ezra accomplished the spiritual establishment of the new community, whereas Nehemiah succeeded in giving it physical stability...The project (building the wall) was completed in the remarkably short time of 52 days.

"During this endeavor, Nehemiah faced determined opposition: mockery (Neh 2:19, 4:1-3), armed raids (4:7-12), a ruse to draw him outside the city, without doubt to murder him (6:1-4), blackmail (6:5-9); and finally, a prophet hired to foretell his death. In every case he met the challenge with courage, wisdom, and

an invincible determination to complete

the task for which God had called him."³

(Falwell 1988)

What happened to transform Nehemiah's heart;
propelling him to hear God's call, heed the call and
have the fortitude to complete the task against so much
opposition?

NEHEMIAH, The Man

The book of Nehemiah begins with his receiving
news from his brother who had come to the palace at
Shushan. He saw him passing by and with excitement,
asked him concerning the people in Jerusalem. "How
were they all doing?" He most likely thought he would
here good news. However, the visitors replied: *"The*

---

³ Jerry Falwell, ed., *The Liberty Annotated Study Bible*,
(Nashville, TN: Thomas Nelson,1988),776

remnant that are left of the captivity there in the province are in great affliction and reproach; the wall of Jerusalem also is broken down, and the gates thereof are burned with fire" (Nehemiah 1:3). How did Nehemiah respond to the news? *"And it came to pass, when I heard these words, that I sat down and wept, and mourned certain days, and fasted, and prayed before the God of heaven"* (Nehemiah 1:4).

Suddenly, Nehemiah was broken hearted for his people. No, longer could he enjoy the comforts of his own life, knowing the suffering of the few, the faithful who had returned to Jerusalem. This certainly was not what he had expected when he ran up to ask his brother how things were going. Obviously, he had not been in touch with his brother. So, easily we live in our bubble of contentment within our own lives; never concerning ourselves with what is going on in our own nation.

Is your heart broken for those who are suffering? Or for the lost? What breaks your heart for the kingdom of God?

What Breaks Your Heart for the Kingdom of God?

The prayer that follows this chance encounter is written out for us in verses 5 to 11 of Nehemiah Chapter 1. That recorded prayer richly holds 7 essential keys for us; to hearing God's call, answering God's call, and finding the fortitude to complete God's call.

Before I embark on detailing those 7 characteristics of his prayer, I would like to address what I believe to be a misconception. Some would try to say that Nehemiah had always been a man of devout prayer or even refer to his prayer as ritualistic; however, I see him as a man content with the status quo of his life. He was content to go about his life with little more than an occasional, "thank you, Lord"; if even that.

Perhaps knowing of God; however, not too concerned otherwise. Much like many Christians today. Happy with their life; occasionally picking up their Bible—at least on Sunday, attending church when it is convenient; and merrily going about their lives until something breaks their heart for God's people.

Ritualistic Prayer? I Think Not, But Some Do

Some look at the first chapter of Nehemiah and assume he was a man already devoted to prayer. However, that idea leads one to question why he had not already returned to Jerusalem. Could it be that God first opened the eyes of Nehemiah's heart that day when he inquired of Hanani "*concerning the Jews that had escaped, which were left of the captivity, and concerning Jerusalem"* (Nehemiah 1:2)?

Gerald A and Chantal Klingbeil argue that Nehemiah's prayer was a ritualistic prayer. They elude to this idea first in a statement within a question. "What triggers Nehemiah's prayer (which should be considered a ritual act) in Neh 1,5-11?"[4] (Klingbeil 2010). The idea is further presented when they describe his response to the sad news as having "triggered a strong ritual response by Nehemiah."[5] These examples infer that Nehemiah had been accustomed to praying in this manner.

A similar sentiment is presented by Richard J. Bautch when he wrote concerning Nehemiah 1:5-11 and Nehemiah 9:32-37: "there is a ceremony of

---

[4] Gerald A Klingbeil and Chantal Klingbeil, "Eyes to hear: Nehemiah 1,6 from a pragmatics and ritual theory perspective," *Biblica 91*, no. 1, 94
[5] Ibid.

covenant renewal. The ceremony is thought to be a crisis ritual."[6] (Bautch 2009) He further declared that "Nehemiah 1:5-11 is a prayer with a clear function to motivate God."[7] However, knowing God is more concerned with a man's heart than his rituals (Psalm 51:16-17, Matthew 5:20); there must be more to Nehemiah's prayer than mere ritual.

KNOWING RITUAL IS NOT ENOUGH

Although, his prayer demonstrates a knowledge of the history of God's Covenant and a familiarity with the scripture; it does not present evidence of his having been accustomed to prayer. Having an intellectual knowledge about scripture does not confirm one as having a close relationship with God, or any relationship with God for that matter. Marc Rasell wrote of the Jewish people being described in Isaiah

---

[6] Richard J. Bautch, *Glory and Power, Ritual and Relationship,* (New York, NY: T&T Clark, 2009), 71
[7] Ibid.,62

1:10-23 as follows: "They called upon the Lord in a ritualistic fashion: fasting, worshipping, praying, observing feasts, and making offerings. The problem was that it was all for themselves. The root of selfishness had not been cured."[8] (Rasell 2012) Perhaps, Nehemiah had never heard or responded to God's Call on his life before that day. Or, perhaps he prayed based on it being "what he should do"; however, never really praying from the depth of his heart, until that day. There was a power much greater in his prayer that day, causing a contented laborer to hear God's call and to say: "yes, Lord, send me: 'thy servant today'" (Nehemiah 1:11).

"The people who returned to the Land of Promise were publicly acknowledging that they believed God would reestablish the nation and usher in

---

[8]Marc Rasell, *Nehemiah The Sabbath Reformer,* (n.p.: lulu.com, 2012), 33, Kindle

a time of kingdom blessing."[9] (Falwell 1988). Yet, Nehemiah had stayed when others had left. He tells us that it was the "twentieth year" (Nehemiah 1:1) of King Artaxerxes reign when he began this prayer. That is clearly "14 years after Ezra's return to Jerusalem."[10] (Falwell 1988)

A CHANGE OF HEART

"Nehemiah could have returned to the land, but for some reason he did not. He took a job instead."[11] (McGee 1982). He held a prestigious position of honor as the "king's cupbearer" (Nehemiah 1:11). In that position, he must have been aware of King Artaxerxes decree, stopping the Jewish people from rebuilding Jerusalem. The decree was written as follows, "*Give ye now commandment to cause these men to cease, and*

---

[9] Falwell, Annotated, 755
[10] Ibid., 776
[11] J. Vernon McGee, Through the Bible with J. Vernon McGee: Volume II Joshua-Psalms, (Nashville, TN: Thomas Nelson, 1982), 503

that this city be not builded, until another
commandment shall be given from me" (Ezra 4:21).
There is no evidence, Nehemiah wept for his people
then. In fact, Nehemiah confesses, *"I had not been*
beforetime sad in his (King Artaxerxes) presence"
(Nehemiah 2:1).

He had never before been sad in the presence of
the king; not even when the King halted the building
the Jerusalem. Yet, Nehemiah, now broken hearted for
his people; turns to God to pray. Chuck Swindoll wrote
about Nehemiah's problem as follows: "The Lord is the
Specialist we need for these 'uncrossable' and
impassable experiences. He delights in accomplishing
what we cannot pull off. But He awaits our cry."[12]
(Swindoll 1998)

---

[12] Chuck Swindoll, *Hand Me Another Brick,* Revised ed.,
Nashville, TN: Word (A Thomas Nelson Company), 1998, 34.

CONCLUDING THOUGHTS

In the next chapter, we will go deeper into that prayer of Nehemiah and the 7 essential characteristics found there to help anyone hear God's call, heed God's call and have the fortitude to complete God's call. God needed Nehemiah to build the wall. He had been chosen; but, before Nehemiah would heed that command, God broke his heart with a burden for the people.

CHAPTER 3:

Serving God with All Your Heart

God commanded Nehemiah to rebuild the wall, as prophesied by Isaiah in Isaiah 9:10. God had prophesized that the wall would be rebuilt, even before Nebuchadnezzar destroyed the wall. However, Nehemiah had no clue he was going to be chosen; until, God broke Nehemiah's heart one fate filled day. He did this first by opening this young cupbearer's heart to see the devastation surrounding His people.

Before that, Nehemiah lived a somewhat plush life as King Artaxerxes cupbearer. Now, his call took him out of that comfort zone. He would be forced to face many harsh enemies. Before, he fully understood the call; broken hearted, he prayed for many days.

What is needed to serve God with all your heart? We gain insight into just that by examining Nehemiah's prayer. Within his prayer, we find seven key elements necessary to hear God's call, heed God's call, and the fortitude to see it through to completion; regardless, of the opposition we may face.

Some Christians remain very content with their positions in life, never seeking to discover God's bigger plan of service for them. What changes a man's heart to make him willing to leave everything familiar behind, face whatever trials confront him, and go into full service for God?

Every Christian is at some point called to serve God. Often it is inconvenient, calling us to leave that which is comfortable to embark on a very treacherous journey confronted by mountains too daunting to consider. However, nothing is too difficult for God.

The seven elements, found in Nehemiah's prayer are what you and I need as well. They are:

compassion, vision, conviction (leading to repentance), humility, submission, commitment, and faith.

Compassion

The book of Nehemiah begins with his asking Hanani about the Jews who had escaped captivity and returned to their home. They responded by telling him that the people *"are in great affliction and reproach: the wall of Jerusalem also is broken down and the gates thereof are burned with fire"* (Nehemiah 1:2). Hearing those words broke his heart.

He tells us in verse four that he wept and mourned for many days. Broken hearted by the news, he wept; and then, turned to God for an answer. What could he, a cupbearer, do? He wasn't a priest or a king. Instead, he was a laborer. How could God use him?

In an exposition concerning Nehemiah, Alexander MacLaren aptly declared:

God prepares His servants for their work by laying on their souls a sorrowful realisation of the miseries which other men regard, and they themselves have often regarded, very lightly. The men who have been raised up to do great work for God and men, have always to begin by greatly and sadly feeling the weight of the sins and sorrows which they are destined to remove. No man will do worthy work at rebuilding the walls who has not wept over the ruins.[13] (MacLaren 2013)

Until one's heart becomes broken for that which breaks God's heart, there is no hope for commitment to complete any task God calls one to. Christians must

---

[13] Alexander MacLaren, *MacLaren Expositions of Holy Scripture: A Reformer's Schooling,* (Dallas, TX: Graceworks Multimedia, March 9, 2013), 187.

first weep for the lost before they can passionately go out "to seek and save those who are lost" (paraphrase of Luke 19:10). True compassion will drive one to their knees in earnest prayer to the only one who can "supply all our needs" (paraphrase from Philippians 4:19).

Until one's heart becomes broken for that which breaks God's heart, there is no hope for commitment to complete any task God calls one to

---

Vision

Compassion alone cannot propel one to action without also having a clear vision of God and his plan for humanity. Nehemiah begins his prayer with,

"O LORD God of heaven, the great and terrible God, that keepeth covenant and mercy for them that love him and observe his commandments" (Nehemiah 1:5). In this opening, Nehemiah declares both who God is and His plan for mankind. So, the vision is two-fold: a vision of who God is and a vision of His plan for mankind.

Of Who God IS:

God is the Almighty, Sovereign, Lord. He is the creator of Heaven and Earth. The great I AM for which nothing exists without Him.

As I wrote in *Abiding, Steadfast Joy:* "The essence of everything begins with God who IS the creator, controller, majestic ruler of the Universe. Outside of His Being, there is nothingness. With that truth, I realize I am nothing until I am found in Him who breaths into me, life. He who created me, formed me in my mother's womb: knew me before He created the earth. Think about that. My very existence is because of His Being the Great I AM.[14] (Barba 2017) This is what Paul meant when he stood on Mars Hill and spoke to the men of Athens, ""*For in him we live, and move, and have our being*" (Acts 17:28).

Until the Christian fully recognizes his or her nothingness before the great I AM; they labor in vain. "*Except the LORD build the house, they labour in vain that build it: except the LORD keep the city, the watchman waketh but in vain*" (Psalm 127:1).

Of God's Plan for Mankind:

Beyond having a vision for who God IS, one must also have a vision of God's Plan for Mankind. Nehemiah recognized God's covenantal love and mercy for those who seek Him. When God called Moses to lead His people, He told Moses of His Name being

---

[14] Effie Darlene Barba, *Abiding, Steadfast Joy*, (Columbia, MO: Effie de Barba Publishing, 2017), 17

Yahweh: I AM. (Exodus 3:14). Furthermore, God said, *"I have surely seen the affliction of my people which are in Egypt, and have heard their cry by reason of their taskmasters; for I know their sorrows; And I am come down to deliver them"* (Exodus 3:7-8).

Following this comes a series of God's responses to every question that Moses brings, "I will. I will be your voice. I will deliver my people. I AM will do it." Recognizing this, Nehemiah next prays, *"Let thine ear now be attentive, and thine eyes open, that thou mayest hear the prayer of thy servant"* (Neh. 1:6).

When God hears the cry of His people earnestly praying, He responds with *"My counsel shall stand, and I will accomplish all my purpose"* (Isaiah 46:10). For, *"God is not a man, that he should lie; neither the son of man that he should repent: hath He said, and shall He not do it?"* (Numbers 23:19)

GOD's PLAN OF SALVATION –

THROUGHOUT THE AGES

With great mercy and love; God never turns His back fully from His redemptive plan.   From the moment He promised Adam and Eve in Genesis 3:15 that He would send salvation into the world God has steadied His hand, withholding the final judgment. He sent His own son into the world to save the world. Furthermore, having provided the means of salvation; He patiently bids all who would believe, to come. He does this because of His great love and mercy.

"For God so loved the world, that He sent His only begotten Son, that whosoever believeth in him should not perish, but have everlasting life. For God sent not his Son into the world to condemn the world; but that the world through him might be saved. He that

35

believeth on him is not condemned: but he that believeth not is condemned already, because he hath not believed in the name of the only begotten Son of God. And this is the condemnation, that light came into the world, and men loved darkness rather than light, because their deeds were evil" (John 3:16-19).

So, the first question is: Do you know Jesus Christ as your Savior and Lord? Then, for all who believe; comes question two: "Are you ready to serve Him with all your life, your heart and your soul?"

THE PLACE GOD CALLS YOU TO:

Frederick Buechner once wrote, "The place God calls you to is the place where your deep gladness and the world's deep hunger meet."[15] (Buechner 1973) Nehemiah now saw the despair in Jerusalem and it broke his heart. He could no longer be happy as the cupbearer. His only hope for happiness was to go where God calls him to serve; regardless of the danger he faced. Furthermore, He fully recognized God as the great I AM who has a plan of salvation for His people. All who would seek Him, calling upon His name; would be eternally saved by faith.

WANTED: One Humbled, Repentant Heart

The remnant of true worshippers of God, had returned to Jerusalem; just as God promised they would in Isaiah, Jeremiah, and Zephaniah. However, they met grave opposition. Their streets had been

---

[15]Frederick Buechner, *Wishful Thinking: A Theological ABC*, (New York: Harper & Row, 1973), 95.

invaded by people of many ideologies. Although, they built their temple; it was openly an easy target. The wall lay in shambles surrounding the city and the gates were destroyed.

King Artaxerxes had ordered them cease their building; because, rebellious oppositional forces sent a false, evil report to him. Their only hope: to build a wall. The wall: a symbol of hope, protection, national pride and that God was on their side; was desperately needed. God chose Nehemiah, to build that wall. God needed a repentant, humbled heart; submitted to serve Him, regardless of the cost.

We began examining Nehemiah's prayer in Nehemiah chapter one, versus 5-11. Within that prayer lies key elements necessary for any Christian to go where ever God might send them to whatever task He might assign them, regardless of the danger ahead or the comfort left behind. The first two of the seven elements found with Nehemiah's prayer, I presented were Compassion and Vision.

Until one's heart breaks for the lost or the dear Children of God who face oppression; I daresay, no one desires to leave the comfortable place they reside in. Ah, but when God opens that heart, fills it with His love and compassion for the lost; then, that one is restless until they answer God's call.

Beyond compassion, they must also have a clear vision of who God is as the great I AM and a vision of His plan of Love to spread the gospel message. Now, let's look at the next three elements found in that prayer.

Conviction, Leading to Repentance

The clearer one's vision of God becomes, the greater one's own sin appears.

The Clearer One's Vision of God becomes, the greater one's own sin appears.

As Leslie Allen wrote: "Repentance is the keynote of the prayer. Although their God was great and awesome, they had disobeyed his commands. That divine greatness made human guilt more reprehensible."[16] (Allen 1995) Recognizing God's just and righteous nature, Nehemiah turns to repentance.

> *I pray before thee now, day and night, for the children of Israel thy servants, and confess the sins of the children of Israel, which we have sinned against thee: both I and my father's house have sinned. We have dealt very corruptly against thee, and have not kept the commandments, nor the statutes, nor the judgments, which thou commandedst thy servant Moses.* (Nehemiah 1:6-7)

A truly repentant heart is necessary to come before a Holy God with our petition. Only then can one understand the depth of grace with which God deals

---

[16] Leslie C. Allen and Timothy S. Laniak, *Ezra, Nehemiah, Esther,* (Grand Rapids, MI: Baker Books, 1995), 143

with his children. Deserving nothing, God gives to his children, everything.

Humility

Once a heart is broken by compassion, gains a true vision of God in all his glory, realizes the depth of his grace, and falls before him in genuine repentance for one's sin; that heart can be nothing less than a humbled heart. Humility opens a man or woman's heart to give grace to others. Realizing that without grace, no one can stand before a righteous God; Nehemiah had prayed for his people and his family. He did not feel superior or prideful; because, he had a clear vision of his own sinful nature.

Humility opens a man or woman's heart to give grace to others.

"He humbled himself before the "God of Heaven" and confessed openly and frankly all sins of the nation, his own sins included."[17] (Swift 1917) Humbled, broken hearted before an Almighty God; Nehemiah asks for grace for himself and his people.

He acknowledged his own and the nations spiritual poverty before God, deserving nothing; yet, he pleads God's own words of grace. *"But if ye turn unto me, and keep my commandments, and do them; though there were of you cast out unto the uttermost part of the heaven, yet will I gather them from thence, and will bring them unto the place that I have chosen to set my name there"* (Nehemiah 1:9).

---

[17] Charles Henry Swift, "Prayer a Vitalizing Force: The Lesson in Today's Life," *The Christian Century,* no 44, November 1, 1917, 16

Submission

The only thing left to do is to submit to God's will; no matter what that might be. No longer could Nehemiah be content in his former life as a cupbearer. "Nehemiah is willing and wants to be used of God. But he is not running ahead of God; he prays about it. He says, 'If you want to use me, I am making myself available.'"[18] (McGee 1982) The prayer changes. "The petition, then, is not merely that I may patiently suffer God's will but also that I may vigorously do it....'Thy will be done-by me-now'"[19] (Lewis 1964)

---

[18] McGee, Through the Bible: Volume II, 506

[19] C. S. Lewis, Letters to Malcolm Chiefly on Prayer: Reflections on the Intimate Dialogue Between Man and God, (Orlando, FL: Harcourt, 1964), 26

Chapter 4:

Faith and Commitment to Finish Well

In the center of Nehemiah's prayer lies the seven necessary elements needed by each Christian to hear God's call, follow God's call (regardless of the cost), and the fortitude to see the task through to completion. Thus far, I have presented the first five keys: 1) compassion resulting from a heart that is broken for the oppressed and lost in the world; 2) a vision of God as the great I AM plus a vision of His plan of salvation for mankind; 3) conviction leading to repentance; 4) humility from realizing His magnitude of grace toward us; and 5: submission to His will. Next, we will look at commitment and faith.

Nehemiah was called to leave the comfort in which he had been living to face danger, opposition, and hard manual labor. This would require a commitment which never looks back or doubts. When others had returned to Jerusalem, he had stayed behind. Now, God called upon him to build a wall.

The wall: a necessary symbol of hope and confirmation of God's protection for the nation. Were he to fail in this mission, the people lay open to siege, both physical and emotional. The wall symbolized their separation from false ideologies and idolatry.

Even though, they once had a wall; they had chosen to allow in dangerous ideas, false religions, and evil by opening their gates. Now, as they turned their eyes back to God. They needed a new fortified wall as a symbol of their separateness from the evils of the world around them. The completion of this wall was paramount to the nation having the heart to stand once more as a nation; instead, of living with a sense of shame and guilt before the world.

Commitment

What had begun as a broken heart for the suffering of God's people; has through prayer reached the place of full surrender and submission to God's will. Now, Nehemiah would need the commitment and fortitude to complete the task; whatever it might be. Commitment often means a life of self-sacrifice, as it certainly did for Nehemiah. He would have to leave everything familiar and go out into the unknown, trusting God. As McLaren wrote:

> such sympathy should be the parent of a noble, self-sacrificing life. Look at the man in our text (Nehemiah). He had the ball at his feet. He had the entrée of a court, and the ear of a king. Brilliant prospects were opening before him, but his brethren's sufferings drew him, and

with a noble resolution of self-sacrifice, he shut himself out from the former and went into the wilderness. He is one of the Scripture characters that never have had due honour--a hero, a saint, a martyr, a reformer. He did, though in a smaller sphere, the very same thing that the writer of the Epistle to the Hebrews magnified with his splendid eloquence, in reference to the great Lawgiver (Moses), 'and chose rather to suffer affliction with the people of God," and to turn his back upon the dazzlements of a court, than to 'enjoy the pleasures of sin for a season,' whilst his brethren were suffering.[20] (MacLaren 2013)

---

[20] MacLaren A Reformer's Schooling, 373

The kind of commitment required to carry the wearied Christian through the trials that come their way requires a willingness to lay it all down for the sake of God's plan; knowing, He is the greater treasure.

Commitment is the willingness to lay it all down for the sake of God's plan; knowing, HE IS the Greatest TREASURE

FAITH

"Faith is knowing, beyond a shadow of doubt; that God IS the great I AM and he rewards those who diligently seek him" (my paraphrase of Hebrews 11:6). Nehemiah now understood the power, magnitude and grace of God. He would trust God for the grace which saved him, the grace to sustain him and the future grace which would present every moment of every day that lay before him along this treacherous journey. As

John Piper so aptly points out "Faith in future grace is the spring of radical righteousness. It's the root of love and all Christ-exalting living."[21] (Piper 1995) Knowing that God holds every future millisecond in his hands of grace; means, trusting him and believing Romans 8:28, no matter how dark the day may seem. *"And we know that all things work together for good to them that love God, to them who are the called according to his purpose."*

CONCLUDING THOUGHTS

Faith in God is necessary to have the commitment to step out into the unknown. How does one gain that kind of faith? Often, it may come through great trials. Learning to lean upon God, no matter what the circumstance before us; can be built amid those tribulations that cause our hearts to turn to God for the

---

[21] John Piper, *Future Grace,* (New York: Multnomah Books, 1995), 322

answer. Then, there are some who need not go through such trials to gain faith. They do so through diligently seeking God in His word and in prayer.

Then there are those, much like Nehemiah. They go through life relatively comfortable; not really planning or thinking much about following God's plan, until, in a flash of one word or sound, their heart breaks. Suddenly, God crashes into their comfortable place and they can do nothing less than to follow Him with all their heart, where ever he leads them to go.

Paul the Apostle was one who diligently fought against God; until, God opened His eyes and allowed Him to see the truth of the gospel. Suddenly, he saw Jesus in all His splendor, as one to be desired above all else. Preaching the gospel lead to His being stoned, imprisoned, and ultimately killed for His faith. Let's look at what Paul wrote concerning the faith to finish well.

Brethren, I count not myself to have apprehended: but this one thing I do, forgetting those things which are behind, and reaching forth unto those things which are before, I press toward the mark for the prize of the high calling of God in Christ Jesus. Let us therefore, as many as be perfect, be thus minded: and if in anything ye be otherwise minded, God shall reveal even this unto you. Philippians 3:13-15

Oh, that we might each of us have the faith to finish the tasks God places before us.

Chapter 5

Dust Mites of The Heart

Nehemiah prayed from a heavy broken heart; uncertain, as to how God would intervene. His final plea before God that day: *"O Lord, I beseech thee, let now thine ear be attentive to the prayer of thy servant, and to the prayer of thy servants, who desire to fear thy name: and prosper, I pray thee, thy servant this day, and grant him mercy in the sight of this man. For I was the king's cupbearer* (Nehemiah 1:11).

Continuing in prayer, he waited. Nowhere are we told that Nehemiah knew God's plan to send him until the day he stood before the king, four months after the first prayer. Four months of praying, waiting and anticipating God's response weighed heavily on Nehemiah.

Waiting reveals the dust mites of our own heart. Wondering, I ask; "Lord, am I the problem. Is my faith too shaky, my hands too unclean, and my heart too insincere, somehow?"

Perhaps for some, waiting causes them to doubt God's ability or His desire to intervene in mankind's dilemmas. Some, even doubt His existence; yet, I daresay there are many, like me; who have come to know Him as the Supreme, Sovereign, Just and Righteous God of love, mercy and grace. Then, when days, months or years pass; awaiting, anticipating God's answer to a prayer: I don't doubt His ability or His desire to bring me good; instead, I examine my own heart.

After all that He has shown me of His Grace, I realize that lurking in the crevices of my heart, bits of dust collect that need to be cleansed once more. Dust mites of pride, doubt, or selfishness; all leading to sin.

Sin crouches at the doorstep of my heart. Somehow, I don't think Nehemiah fully knew God's plan while he waited; because, those who wait knowing God's plan, aren't so burdened.

DUST MITES OF THE HEART

In this fallen world, dust and cobwebs can be found in the cleanest of homes. One moment of inattention to cleaning, they increase with a rapidity that seems unbelievable. The same is true of our hearts. When, we lay aside our Bibles, become too contented to pray, or allow other things to take God's rightful time in our hearts; dust mites and cobwebs grow within our hearts.

*When we become so content that we lay aside
our Bibles and Prayer, dust mites and cobwebs
grow in our hearts.*

Then, when God places us in the waiting room, the light of His truth shines in revealing all the dust mites and cobwebs needing to be cleansed. During that time of waiting for His answer, He bids us to lay every sin of thought and deed at the foot of the cross, in full surrender to His will. He will cleanse our heart, sweeping away every dust mite of pride, anger, selfishness, and the cobwebs of our doubt.

So, Nehemiah waited; while God fully cleansed and prepared his heart for the task ahead. We know that to be the case; because, when the fateful day that God revealed His plan, Nehemiah's countenance was very sad. Once one knows for certain God's precise plan, there is no place for sadness. The depth of his sorrow lets us know, Nehemiah did not yet know with certainty God's plan. So, we arrive at the day of its revealing.

ONE SAD SERVENT, A KING, AND GOD'S PLAN REVEALED

And it came to pass in the month Nisan, in the twentieth year of Artaxerxes the king, that wine was before him: and I took up the wine, and gave it unto the king.

Now I had not been beforetime sad in his presence. Wherefore the king said unto me, "Why is thy countenance sad, seeing thou art not sick? this is nothing else but sorrow of heart." Then I was very sore afraid,

And said unto the king, "Let the king live forever: why should not my countenance be sad, when the city, the place of my fathers' sepulchres, lieth waste, and the gates thereof are consumed with fire?"

Then the king said unto me, "For what dost thou make request?" So, I prayed to the God of heaven.

And I said unto the king, "If it please the king, and if thy servant has found favour in thy sight, that thou wouldest send me unto Judah, unto the city of my fathers' sepulchres, that I may build it." Moreover, I said unto the king, "If it please the king, let letters be given me to the governors beyond the river, that they may convey me over till I come

into Judah; And a letter unto Asaph the
keeper of the king's forest that he may
give me timber to make beams for the
gates of the palace which appertained to
the house, and for the wall of the city,
and for the house that I shall enter into."
And the king granted me according to
the good hand of my God upon me.
(Nehemiah 2:1-7).

Note that Nehemiah was afraid when the king
noticed his sorrow. Another clue that Nehemiah was
not certain of God's plan yet. However, as he began to
tell the king the reason of his sorrow, light bulbs began
to go off in his heart and mind. Wasn't this what he
had asked God for months ago, to find mercy before the
king? Ah, but all the cleansing of his heart that God
accomplished during that four months causes
Nehemiah to pray; before, he tells King Artaxerxes:

"send me to build the wall." Yet, look at the difference; now, suddenly Nehemiah boldly asks for everything he will need, and he is granted all that he asks for. Nehemiah knows this is an act of grace by God Himself.

GOD'S PLAN: BUILD THAT WALL

Over the course of the four months, God had prepared the heart of Nehemiah to be the one to accomplish His plan. Most likely, Nehemiah was shocked that God was sending him to build the wall. However, whom better to send? He had seen the beautiful structure of the walls surrounding the palace. Furthermore, as cupbearer to the king; he had a position of prestige. Beyond that, most importantly; God had prepared his heart while in the waiting room of God. There, God had dusted away the dust mites and swept away all the cobwebs, so Nehemiah was prepared to face the opposition and trials that lay ahead of him.

CONCLUSION:

Does God have you in His waiting room? Are there prayers, you are awaiting an answer? Lay open your heart before God, knowing He has a perfect plan for you; when, you seek Him.

For I know the thoughts that I think toward you, saith the Lord, thoughts of peace, and not of evil, to give you an expected end. Then shall ye call upon me, and ye shall go and pray unto me, and I will hearken unto you. And ye shall seek me, and find me, when ye shall search for me with all your heart. And I will be found of you, saith the Lord: and I will turn away your captivity, Jeremiah 29:11-14

So, when the world seems hard, or you feel captive to your circumstances or sin; seek Him and search for Him. His promise: " I will be found, and I will turn away your captivity. Then, as He prepares and cleanses your heart, keep your eyes fixed on Him. Trust Him; because, He is faithful and will accomplish all that He has planned.

Also, it is during those waiting moments; you might want to go back and refresh your memory of the three foundations of truth needed to always live a life of Abiding, Steadfast Joy. These I outlined for you in my book of the same title. Truths I learned over a lifetime of waiting rooms. 1. Know your place in the Universe (Hebrews 11:6) 2. Your purpose (John 17). And your position (identity) in Christ Jesus (Ephesians 1-3).

Chapter 6

Is Compromise Truly Loving?

So, it was that Nehemiah began his journey. King Artaxerxes presented him with letters of commendation and an army force to assist him in his journey. Additionally, he was provided with letters so that he might be provided with wood from the king's forest to assist in the rebuilding of the wall. Despite the king's assistance, Nehemiah would face great opposition every step of his journey.

Willingly, he left the comfort of his prestigious position to face hardship; because, he held fast to God's truth. He would not compromise or adopt their ideologies to win their favor. His only hope: God was with him, guiding and leading him. Love demanded he take a stand for God as the supreme Lord and King of the universe. He would take a stand for truth;

63

regardless of the oppositions' attacks, even upon his own life. Resolved to accomplish God's plan; because, true love demanded him to do so.

All too often, in our attempts to demonstrate love; the church has been willing to compromise the truth of the gospel message. Believing that by thus doing, we are moving into a new era of love. However, when in the name of love, we fail to address man's plight as a sinner, separated from God's love because of sin: we fail to love at all.

If indeed, my greatest treasure is an intimate relationship with God, obtained by grace alone through faith in Jesus Christ; then, my most unloving act would be to not take a stand for that truth. When, I join in the forces of those calling for truth to be relative to our ever-changing society; then, I have failed to love. To truly love, I must in meekness and humility reach out a hand; proclaiming God's truth as presented in the gospel.

THE DANGERS OF COMPROMISE:

THE OUTCRY OF MODERNISM

Many in society attempt to declare that the gospel message or that the Bible is outdated. We are told that we must compromise to keep pace with our modern society; because of all the advancements. Yet, even as Ecclesiastes points out: *"The thing that hath been, it is that which shall be; and that which is done is that which shall be done: and there is no new thing under the sun"* (Ecclesiastes 1:9).

The fact that God allows mankind to discover more of what he formerly did not know; does not make it new. The rotation of the earth around the sun. The far and distant galaxies before unseen were there from the time of creation. Just because we had not discovered all; did not mean they were not there. There remains one truth: God. Beyond that, there remains the truth of mankind's fall; because, humans desired and still do desire to be their own gods.

Mankind continues to search for meaning out of nothingness. Placing their faith in an improbability; they declare everything came about due to evolution, for which we remain evolving. Yet, evolution provides no explanation for consciousness, reasoning, nor the innate desire of men and women for meaning and purpose. Only, the scripture supplies a plausible explanation; in that man was created in "the image of God." Nor, can evolution explain evil. Evil presents as the absence of righteousness; because men choose to deny God through declaring themselves as gods or the forger of their own destiny.

SARTRE'S DEATHBED CONFESSION:

Jean Paul Sartre, a staunch atheist well known for his declarations that man is, by his actions, whomever he chooses to be. He believed that out of existence, ultimately comes meaning and being, when one strives for it. Yet, a few months prior to his death; he began to question his lifelong ideas. After having made such an impact on modern man's self-determination and promotion of atheism, on his deathbed he is quoted as saying, "I do not feel that I am the product of chance, a speck of dust in the universe, but someone who was expected, prepared, prefigured. In short, a being only a Creator could put here; and this idea of a creating hand is God."[22] (Zacharias 2008). Once more I have somewhat jumped ahead; because, we will delve much deeper into these ideas in the second section of the book. However,

---

[22] [1]Ravi Zacharias, *The End of Reason,* (Grand Rapids, MI: Zondervan, 2008), 43 see endnotes

here it stands to help introduce the next step of Nehemiah's journey.

NEHEMIAH-NO COMPROMISE ON TRUTH

So, it is Nehemiah left all the comforts behind, to go and build the wall. He would face forces who proclaimed: "We believe in the same God as you, join hands with us." Yet, he knew there was no room to compromise on truth. Those proclaiming this embraced a modernized view of God, embracing idol worship alongside their faith, which in truth was no faith in the God of scripture. What about us? Are we willing to compromise the truth in the name of "tolerance and love"? Or will we stand on the truth of the gospel message, regardless of the criticism and hardship our stance may bring?

God's Hand is Stretched Out Still

Isaiah had spoken of the wall being rebuilt in Isaiah 9: 10. *"The bricks are fallen down, but we will build with hewn stones."* This prophecy was declared in Isaiah long before God commanded Nehemiah to "build that wall." The prophecy came before the wall was even destroyed by Nebuchadnezzar. Yet, three times in Isaiah 9, it is written: *"For all this his anger is not turned away, but his hand is stretched out still"* (verses 12, 17, and 21). God's hand is stretched out still, bidding all who will come to accept His gift of salvation.

Also in Isaiah 9:6, we are told of Jesus. *"For unto us a child is born, unto us a child is given: and the government shall be upon His shoulder: and His name shall be called Wonderful, Counselor, The Mighty God, The everlasting Father, The Prince of Peace."*

So, will we compromise in the name of love; or will we truly love, by standing firm upon the truth of the gospel. We face the same opposition today that Nehemiah did. Will we compromise truth for a lie? Or will we hold firm to the truth of Scripture.

Will we compromise truth, in the name of love and tolerance; or will we truly love by standing firm on the truth of the gospel?

Chapter 7

The True Significance of a Wall

Nehemiah's journey had taken over two months. Finally, he arrived into Jerusalem. Along the way, he was protected by the army of King Artaxerxes. He presented letters to the governors who assisted his journey, and to the keeper of the king's forests to provide him with the needed timber to build the wall. (Nehemiah 2:8). Many who opposed him heard of his plans and were angered.

The wall would be a renewed symbol of strength and proof of God's protecting hand of grace upon His people. Despite the opposition (many proclaiming themselves worshippers of God) having halted the building project through their letters to King Artaxerxes many years earlier; God had now sent Nehemiah with one command: "Build that Wall".

Remember, their letters had led to the king's decree to cease all building years before. (Ezra 4:21-23). Now, Nehemiah arrived with letters to proceed from the very same king; accompanied by the king's army. Nehemiah entered the city. What was so significant about building the wall? Why had there been such opposition to it in the past? The wall would provide protection for Jerusalem and would symbolized their uniqueness as a nation under God's protective hand.

Upon his arrival, Nehemiah waited three days. Most likely, days spent in prayer and surveying the skills of the people. He did not tell them of his plans to rebuild the wall. Then, after three days he went out at night to survey the project. Riding a donkey, he surveyed the ruins; developing a plan. There was an area so covered with debris it forced Nehemiah to dismount; because, the donkey could not walk through.

Imagine the size of this project. However, as a leader; Nehemiah developed a plan for the building. He knew God could complete the work; no matter, how difficult or impossible it appeared. God is a God of the impossible: after all, it was God's Grace that had brought him to this place at this time to accomplish this plan of building the wall.

WHY BUILD A WALL?

After he carefully surveyed the wall, most likely considering who would be needed for each part of the project; he was ready to present his plan. He gathered together all the people and said:

> *"Then said I unto them. Ye see the distress that we are in, how Jerusalem lieth waste, and the gates thereof are burned with fire: come, let us build up the wall of Jerusalem, that we be no more a reproach. Then, I told them of the*

hand of my God which was good unto me; as also the king's words that he had spoken unto me. And they said, 'Let us rise up and build.' So, they strengthened their hands for this good work" *(Nehemiah 2:17-18).*

"First, he challenged them to notice their deplorable circumstances, which had brought them **trouble** and **disgrace** (cf. 1:3). Then he challenged them to **rebuild the wall of Jerusalem,** and followed his challenge with a personal testimony as to how God's **gracious hand** (cf. 2:8) had granted him favor before King Artaxerxes. [23] (Getz 2004)

The wall was needed to protect them from their enemies, to be a reminder of God's grace toward them,

---

[23] Gene A. Getz, "Nehemiah", *The Bible Knowledge Commentary: An Exposition of the Scriptures by Dallas Seminary Faculty-Old Testament,* eds. John F. Woolvard and Roy B. Zuck, (Colorado Springs, CO: Victor, 2004), 677

and to protect them from evil entering their cities and their hearts. The wall symbolized their sovereignty as a nation. It was the one thing that could lift their despairing hearts to stand strong once more in the world as a nation.

DO WE NEED A WALL?

Isaiah foretold of the people's cry, *"the Lord hath forsaken me, and my Lord hath forgotten me"* (Isaiah 49:14). To this God replied:

> *"Behold, I have graven thee upon the palms of my hands; thy walls are continually before me. Thy children shall make hast; thy destroyers and they that made thee waste shall go forth of (go away from) thee* (Isaiah 49:16-17).

Just as the wall was needed to protect the nation; we need a wall about our hearts. We need a wall built by God through diligent Bible Study, prayer, and communion with God. As Chuck Swindoll wrote in *Hand Me Another Brick:*

> "Quite frankly, I think the walls of our lives often lie in ruins through neglect. The leader who brings us to rebuild the walls is the Holy Spirit, and it is He who continues the work of reconstruction inside us. He tries His best to bring to our attention the condition of our walls, but sometimes we don't hear what He is saying. We are not hard of hearing; we simply don't listen.
>
> Some of you are living within the walls of your life surrounded by ruin, and it all began very slowly. First there was a loose piece of stone or mortar. Then there was a crack that appeared in the wall. And

then it broke into pieces, and there was a hole. Because of further neglect, the weeds of carnality began to grow through the wall. By and by, the enemy gained free access to your life."[24] (Swindoll 1998)

When we forsake the walls around our heart, soon they will lie in rubles around us and the enemy will find easy access.

REBUILDING YOUR BROKEN WALL

The only way to rebuild and maintain the wall you need to survive in this journey is daily bible study

---

[24] Chuck Swindoll, *Hand Me Another Brick,* Revised ed., Nashville, TN: Word (A Thomas Nelson Company), 1998, 15

and prayer. How quickly we proclaim, "I don't have time. Or, I am in just a different stage of life. Other excuses, "I just can't concentrate." Then, we wonder what happened when our life lies in ruble around us. God has promised to protect us, *"thy walls are continually before me."* Although, Jerusalem's wall was in shambles; because, of their allowing so much evil and idolatry to enter their city, their nation, and their heart. Still God sent Nehemiah to rebuild the wall. Their wall was always before Him. He knew how important that wall really was.

God has sent the Holy Spirit to maintain and to rebuild that wall of protection around your heart; but, you must heed His call. You must set aside a time for God every day. Set your alarm a little earlier, just to be with God. Study His word. Spend time with Him in prayer. Take time to fellowship with the Lord; so the

Holy Spirit can maintain the protective wall around your heart and mind.

OPPOSITION TO BUILDING A WALL

Oh, there will be opposition. Some will say you are ritualistic and God hates ritual. Ah, but you see a habit is not the same as a ritual. Many years ago, due to a chronic illness awakening me with pain; I was forced to get up early. I began spending those early hours studying and reading my Bible. Those hours in His Word and in prayer were what carried me through an impossible time.

Today, I still get up early every morning; because, I know I can't face the day ahead without Him. He is the strength, the hope and the protector I need. I know how easy my heart can be swayed to pride, self-exaltation, sorrow, depression and sin; if I neglect time spent with Him, the walls around my heart will soon lie in rubles around me.

Nehemiah's opposition protested immediately, proclaiming that he was going against the king. His answer?

"The God of heaven, he will prosper us; therefore, we his servants will arise and build: but ye have no portion, nor right, nor memorial, in Jerusalem" (Nehemiah 2:20).

So, when Satan tells you that you don't need to get up early to be with God; remind him, he has no place reserved for him in heaven.

Chapter 8

Facing the Opposition

Nehemiah gathered all the people, divided the job into sections and began the work of building the wall. The task was immense. For that reason, until this time, the people had seen it as impossible. They needed a leader who could break it down into sections; therefore, God sent Nehemiah. With each group assigned a small section, the task now suddenly appears doable.

It is that way with most of the work you face. Looking at the whole task, one tends to sit down in desperation; however, by breaking it into pieces, one gains new hope and invigoration to get the job done. But opposition presented itself quickly; beginning with mockery and demoralizing jabs.

Whenever one marches forward to do God's work in this world, opposition arises. Satan places many roadblocks to cross. How does one combat opposition from without and from within one's own heart?

Those opposing the wall began with mockery. Sanballat began. "What does this bunch of poor, feeble Jews think they are doing? He scoffed. 'do they think they can build the wall in a day if they offer enough sacrifices? And look at those charred stones they are pulling out of the rubbish and using again!' Tobiah, who was standing beside him, remarked, 'If even a fox walked along the top of their wall, it would collapse!" (Nehemiah 4:2-3, TLB).

In other words, "you bunch of weak, incompetent fools. You think God really is going to help you? Besides that, look at all that ruble and garbage! Even if you build it, it will fall down again."

COMBAT OPPOSITION WITH TRUTH

The enemy, as you may recall; weren't worshippers of God, they were foreign diplomats who wanted power. Nehemiah had made this clear, when he replied to their first criticisms: *"The God of heaven will help us succeed. We, his servants, will start rebuilding this wall. But you have no share, legal right, or historic claim in Jerusalem"* (Nehemiah 2:20).

To paraphrase, "unless you bow down before the throne of God to worship Him; you have no say here. This is God's work and His work will be accomplished by Him through we, his servants." In other words, "Get behind me Satan. I will not be deterred in doing God's work. He will provide a way."

Just as a side note to place this all-in perspective. Sanballat, was an opportunist. He, according to Josephus (a historian from the first century A.D.) was a governor over the area. Furthermore, he had convinced the high priest of Judah to go against Gods laws and marry his daughter. He did this to maintain a position of power. He believed that a divided and diverse Israel was a controllable Israel.[25] (Josephus 1998). Although, there are some discrepancies with Josephus' work; he does add some perspective and credence to God's own inspired word.

COMBAT OPPOSITION WITH PRAYER

Sometimes, it is not necessary to speak or to get into a confrontation with the opposition. During those times, pray! Nehemiah knew this battle, was not

---

[25] Josephus, "The Antiquities of the Jews", *Josephus: The Complete Works,* trans. William Whiston, (Nashville, TN: Thomas Nelson Publishers. 1998), pages 366-367

*"against flesh and blood, but against principalities,
against powers, against the rulers of the darkness of
this world, against spiritual wickedness in high
places"* (Ephesians 6:12). And, Nehemiah knew who
had the power to win this battle was God, alone.
Instead of responding to the attacker; this time,
Nehemiah just prayed.

> *"Hear, O our God; for we are despised:
> and turn their reproach upon their own
> head, and give them for a prey in the
> land of captivity: And cover not their
> iniquity, and let not their sin be blotted
> out from before thee: for they have
> provoked thee to anger before the
> builders"* (Nehemiah 4: 4-5).

The opposition had demeaned God and caused
the people to question their faith and their zeal to
perform the task God had called upon them to perform.

God commanded "build that wall!" Yes, we are to pray for the salvation of every soul; however, it is ok to ask God to justly punish evil as well.

We do not always have to come back with a statement. Certainly, we are not to respond with revenge. Sometimes, we need to remain silent and pray. God has a plan and we need to let Him be God, our provider and our protector against the enemy. Oh, but another very important truth is shown here. Don't stop the work He commanded you do, while waiting for God to respond. Keep working. Most likely the opposition is going to get a lot worse; before, it gets better.

COMBAT OPPOSITION FROM WITHIN

Although, many times we may face opposition from without; sometimes, the opposition is within our own mind and heart. Particularly, following a victory. It is at least for me. Recently, I released two new books.

In addition, I am taking classes on line from Liberty University; working toward a master's in theology. Beyond that, I do work full time and continue to maintain and write for this website. Every time I am standing in praise to God (perhaps for His having met a financial need, a spiritual victory, an answered prayer or miraculously the money stretches to the next paycheck). Then, the voices come, Satan whispering, "You fool. God couldn't possibly love you. What a weak, feeble foolish girl you are. Even, if you finished the book; no one will read it. With your history with money; why would God provide you a way? And school, forget that."

My response: "Satan, get out of my way; you have no place here in my sanctuary." Then, I fall before God's throne of grace; knowing, He has a plan and can use this fragile clay pot for His Glory. He will provide a way through today and tomorrow. After that, I get up and continue to march forward. It is not about treasures here on this earth. It is about doing God's

Whatever Opposition You Face today; don't forget to speak truth, pray for God's Guidance, and Keep Marching forward.

will, His way; even if, that is a constant uphill battle; then as Charles Stanley always says, "Leave the consequences to Him."

FINISHING WELL DESPITE ENEMY FIRE

The people continued building the wall; despite, the criticism being launched at them. They had prayed for the enemy to be removed; however, the enemy now more determined, decided to launch a military attack against the builders.

Often, when Satan realizes that his mocking words can't deter the Christian from doing God's work; he launches a greater attack and God allows him to. Not because God didn't hear our prayers, nor because we are outside His Will. God knows what is best. He recognizes our need to grow both in our faith and in our defense system. Our next task may require just that. Besides, He is always at work bringing us to a place of perfect joy in Him. That requires our growing in faith and in trusting Him with the outcomes.

Furthermore, unless we learn how to defend ourselves against the enemy; we cannot accomplish the greatest task at hand: to spread the gospel truth to a world in need of Him. We must act, defending the cause of Christ. So, how do we keep going and finish well, when the Enemy Attacks? To do so we must arm ourselves with the sword of truth.

Remember our battle is *"not against flesh and blood, but against principalities, against powers, against the rulers of the darkness of this world, against spiritual wickedness in high places"* (Ephesians 6:12). God has provided us with His armor to protect us. The only weapon He gave us is: *"the Sword of the Spirit, which is the Word of God"* (Ephesians 6:17). This is a powerful sword in two ways. It is the truth of the gospel message and it is the power of Christ in us. To wield this sword or to stand firm when the enemy attacks, we must *"study to show (ourselves) approved unto God, a workman that needeth not to be ashamed, rightly dividing the word of truth"* (2 Timothy 2:15). Always be prepared for battle; because, it is certain that the opposition will attack if we are doing God's work.

WHEN THE OPPOSITION ATTACKS

So, it was that the enemies opposing the wall; planned a military attack. Their plan: surround the people working on the wall and stop the builders through brute force. The people discouraged, suddenly saw the task as too great. They became afraid when they heard of the planned attack. Listen to their words:

And Judah said, *"The strength of the bearers of burdens is decayed, and there is much rubbish: so that we are not able to build the wall. And our adversaries said, 'They shall not know, neither see, till we come in the midst among them, and slay them, and cause the work to cease'"* (Nehemiah 4:10-11).

The labor for God's Kingdom at times appears impossible. So often, we labor with no signs of reward. The rubbish before us that must be cleared appears too great and the opposition too strong. Discouragement builds within our own hearts; until, we like the people

91

of Jerusalem, desire to cease. Weary from the work, covered with the scars of labor; we see the obstacles before us and we sit down defeated. We return to life, merely going through the motions, turn on the TV; go about work somber, afraid that someone might discover our faith. Our Bible lays on the bedside table or the bookshelf, unopened. After all, if God really wanted us to labor; wouldn't we see the reward now?

ARMED TO KEEP GOING

Undeterred, Nehemiah, a true leader kept his eyes focused on the goal; instead of the obstacles. He rallied the troops and called the weary builders to action by two means.

First, he reminded them, God is on their side and He commanded the wall be built. He will accomplish all that He plans; regardless, of the enemy attacks. In fact, His power and glory will shine through even brighter to the world as He overcomes the enemy attacks; bringing light and truth into the darkness of the enemy's evil and lies.

So, Nehemiah said to all the people, *"Be not afraid of them: remember the Lord, which is great and terrible, and fight for your brethren, your sons, and your daughters, your wives, and your houses"* (Nehemiah 4:14).

Second, he commanded half of the people to stand as guards protecting the builders. Every worker was armed with a sword. Furthermore, he set up an alarm system; whereby, the people were to all join as one unit prepared for battle if they heard the trumpet sound. Then he proclaimed, "You have nothing to fear, *"Our God shall fight for us"* (Nehemiah 4:20).

With the growing enemy army against the Christian faith around the world and even in our own country, don't we hear the trumpet sounding? We must remember God is fighting for us. He has won the final victory, we must continue working and building.

Do not get discouraged!

Chapter 9

GREED AND ABUSE

The building of the wall continued, despite the oppositions plans to secretly attack the workers and slay them. God had allowed their evil plots to become known. Nehemiah placed guards surrounding the workers and, also, armed the workers. He established a plan of notification to alert them when the enemy approaches by developing an alarm system. Do you have an alarm system guarding your heart and mind from the enemy attacks? Arising early, do you spend time in the word and in communion with the Holy Spirit. God has set up the alarm system for us; we need to learn to recognize it.

Therefore, they continued to build the wall at God's command and under His protection. Then the whole project came to a screeching halt as the workers began to grumble. A revolt of sorts; because, they were in financial distress. Not an unusual place to be when truly doing God's work. Yet, their distress had been worsened by the greed and abuse of their fellow Jews. Satan had thus far failed to stop the building by outside opposition, now he tried from within. There needed to be a spiritual cleansing from the inside before the work could continue.

Remember the Jewish people had been slaves, captives for 70 years prior to their return to the land. They had rebuilt the temple and now they were building the wall. Suddenly they remembered their own financial distress. The wall would protect them from external tyranny; however, they faced severe financial stress from their own people. The wall would not protect them from the greed and abuse within their own people. The wall would not provide food for their children or a roof over their own head.

Despite their return to the land, there wasn't enough food to support their families. Over the course of time, while remaining subjects of Persia; they had to pay taxes on their land. Furthermore, to make matters worse; famine hit their land due to drought. To survive, most of the people were forced to borrow from the few Jewish people who had money. This was necessary to survive; however, their own leaders placed high interest on the loans. When they could not pay the interest, they were forced to hand over their land. Some sold their children into slavery to their Jewish nobles.

GREED AND ABUSE RAMPANT WITHIN

With such greed and abuse within the leadership, suddenly the people realized that the wall would not help them overcome the dire poverty they faced. So, what if the wall is finished? Even then, they could not live their lives in peace with so much poverty and financial distress. They halted the work and voiced their distress to Nehemiah. Nehemiah's first response was anger.

> *"I was very angry when I heard their cry and these words. Then I consulted with myself, and I rebuked the nobles, and the rulers, and said unto them, Ye exact usury, every one of his brother. And I set a great assembly against them. And I said unto them, we after our ability have redeemed our brethren the Jews, which were sold unto the heathen: and will ye even sell your brethren? Or shall they be sold unto us? Then held they their peace, and found nothing to answer"* (Nehemiah 5:6-8)

Caught, they had no answer. The Jewish law in Exodus 22:25 forbade them from lending money to the poor to gain profit through interest: *"If thou lend money to any of my people that is poor by thee, thou shalt not be to him a usurer, neither shalt thou lay upon him usury...and when he crieth unto me, that I will hear; for I am gracious."*

How was it that after spending 70 years in exile for the nation's sin, they could be breaking this law of God?

A MEASURED RESPONSE

Note, Nehemiah consulted with himself before speaking. In other words, he did not suddenly respond in anger. Instead, he thought carefully about what he was going to say; then, he responded. After beginning his rebuke, he did so with reminding them of God's laws and God's just nature.

'And I also said, "It is not good that ye do: ought ye not to walk in the fear of

our God because of the reproach of the heathen our enemies?... Restore, I pray you, to them, even this day, their lands, their vineyards, the olive yards, and their houses, also the hundredth part of the money, and of the corn, the wine, and the oil that ye exact of them" *(Nehemiah 5:9, 11).*

Nehemiah then had them all take an oath to return to the people all their possessions and the interest money that had been taken from them. He then shook his garment to symbolize his "shaking off all who would not keep the promise." He then said, *"God shake out every man from his house, and from his labor that performeth not this promise, even thus be he shaken out, and emptied"* (Nehemiah 5:13).

Nehemiah placed the final judgment of the greedy and those who abused their people into God's hands to judge. God frowns upon those leaders who oppress His people because of their greed or abuse in over taxing, as well as those who oppress the people who willingly are working hard to provide for their family.

God Hates Greed and Abuse; He calls upon His people to help the poor without wanting any reward or personal retribution for doing so.

SIN WITHIN MUST BE PURGED

The wall could protect the people from outside threats of tyranny; but, sin within had to be purged. We must be always seeking to follow God's commands and live righteously. God provides for His people all that they need; however, He does ask for obedience to

His commands. As much as we are able, we are to help our neighbors. Not to gain ourselves; rather, to be gracious in the same manner God has been gracious to us.

CHAPTER 10

An Evil Invitation

They had faced the threat of attacks from without and the revolt from within. The wall was completed. All that was left to finish the task was to construct and place the many gates. Sometimes, when we are seeing the end in sight; we become vulnerable to Satan's attacks. Our overflowing joy, opens us up as an easy target. Feeling exuberant as nothing can stop us now; we begin our victory dance and let down our guard. Typically, that is when Satan begins a subtle approach.

Nehemiah faced the same. He must have sighed in relief and danced with joy to God, when the walls stood completed. Now to finish the gates. Still a formidable task; yet, with great joy and hope the workers moved forward. That was when Nehemiah received an invitation from Sanballat to come out to a beautiful valley retreat and meet with him.

It would seem the reasonable; and perhaps a kind thing to do. Go out and meet with your former opposition; after all, they had failed to stop you. God is on your side and the proper Christian thing to do would be to extend a hand of friendship by accepting the invitation. "Come, let us meet; that, we might work out a compromise."

To this, Nehemiah said, "No! I have way too much work here to yet accomplish." He realized the truth. Their invitation wasn't really to have a nice little meeting, nor were they concerned with Nehemiah's wellbeing. They were not really offering him a getaway retreat. Instead they were plotting to kill him. If they could get him out of the way, the people would never finish the gates. Without the gates, the walls alone would not protect the people.

AN INVITATION TO COMPROMISE

Within the modern age, we often are faced with many who ask us to compromise on the truth of the gospel. We are urged to be open minded, embracing other religions as possibly being true as well. They say, "after all, if you continue to proclaim that Christ is the only way; aren't you being too narrow minded." An open invitation to meet at the table of compromise, at the negotiating table with the agnostics, atheists, Hindus, Buddhists, Muslims, and the new age (only to name a few). In the name of harmony, our invitation is to compromise on the truth of the gospel message. We are to love all these, and we are not to shut the door; neither, are we to lay aside the truth of the gospel message as being merely relative and unimportant.

We must with great patience and love, defend the truth of the gospel through both our words and our deeds. To truly love our neighbor as our self, demands

105

just that. I cannot truly love someone, while I hold the secret to life, joy, and hope hidden deep within my own heart. Certainly, it is not an act of love to say; "all will be ok, I am certain God will accept all into heaven; regardless of your beliefs." To do so, would be the

To Truly Love Your Neighbor is to hold fast to the truth of the gospel, presenting it by your actions; demonstrating God's Grace, Love and Joy in all that you do or say. To compromise the truth is indeed an act of hate instead.

greatest act of hatred you or I could perpetrate on our neighbor.

AN INVITATION TO TRULY LOVE

Certainly, we are to reach out with gentle, patient hands of love to our neighbors; regardless of their faith. We are not to stand and angrily argue, nor call them names. But we must be prepared to live a life that exemplifies Christ in all that we do or say. We must study God's words and be ready to defend it to a world in need of Him. We must also, through prayer be diligent not to compromise the truth of the gospel. Let the Holy Spirit guide you and assist you when faced with an invitation on how to respond.

2 Peter 3: 15-18

And account that the longsuffering of our Lord is salvation; even as our beloved brother Paul also according to the wisdom given unto him hath written

107

unto you; As also in all his epistles, speaking in them of these things; in which are some things hard to be understood, which they that are unlearned and unstable wrest, as they do also the other scriptures, unto their own destruction. Ye therefore, beloved, seeing ye know these things before, beware lest ye also, being led away with the error of the wicked, fall from your own steadfastness. But grow in grace, and in the knowledge of our Lord and Savior Jesus Christ. To him be glory both now and forever. Amen.

There is no sweeter testimony to Jesus Christ, than the joy, kindness and generosity of His people during the moments of great hardship they may be facing themselves.

Chapter 11

Victory Draws Near

The enemy attacks remain persistent when we are doing the work of the Lord. The greater the work, the nearer its completion; the more ferocious will be the attacks. Satan uses threats, lies, and whatever means he can to cause doubt, disruption, sorrow, and fear.

This was the case for Nehemiah as well. The enemy continued to send invitations to Nehemiah to come, take a break from the work, and meet with them so they could negotiate a plan. When he declined every invitation, they sent a letter filled with false accusations. This letter they failed to seal; because, they wanted to spread these false rumors as quickly as possible. Knowing the hearts of men are so quickly bent to gossip, they purposefully wanted the false accusations to be leaked to the press of the day. (So, fake news was prevalent even in Nehemiah's day) Surely, Sanballat thought, that would cause the people to doubt Nehemiah, bringing about a revolt.

Nehemiah's reply was swift. "Your words are all lies. What you accuse me of are what you, yourself, are guilty of." You see, the letters accused Nehemiah of doing all this to gain fame, fortune, and power over the people of Israel. But, that was what Sanballat had plotted to do. In fact, he had married his daughter to one of the high priests in Jerusalem; so that, he might have influence and power. He knew his daughter would entice the priests to idolatrous worship; that, the power of God within the nation might be thwarted.

Sanballat had seen and heard of God's power; but, did not worship Him. Instead, Sanballat wanted to draw God's people away from God's favor and into His judgement. Then, he knew he could overpower them. Sanballat wanted power at any cost. Funny how that is the case in most false accusations, even today. People who desire power, regardless of the cost to the people around them.

THE ENEMY ATTACKS

Satan knows the power, glory, and majesty of God. Yet, Satan refuses to bow to him; because of his own egotistical love. Remember, he was so egotistical that he even tried to tempt Jesus into disobedience. Such arrogance and deceit often present in the attacks we face as well. When, the critics of the gospel attack; they do so with such lies, arrogance, and an outrageous self-promoting cry of having the moral high ground. Just like Sanballat, they scream accusations of bigotry, point fingers; while the whole time, they are the guilty ones.

So, what did Nehemiah do? He prayed: *"Now therefore, O God, strengthen my hands"* (Nehemiah 6:9). The prayer was short; but, effective.

How often during life, we need just that prayer? When the enemy attacks, our hearts weaken, discouragement sets in, and we fold our hands, bow our

Now therefore, O God, strengthen my hands

Nehemiah 6:9

heads in sorrow. How often have we quit the task before us, just before we gain the victory?   In those moments, my only prayer is: "O God, please strengthen my heart and my hands. Help me to see you and know you want me to go on."

It has been those moments of my greatest doubt that God would send a messenger, someone who helped me to see that I was to continue; regardless, of the enemy attacks. God would strengthen my hands to continue the labor before me.

A CHANGE IN TACTICS

Nehemiah went to visit a "shut in". When he got there, the shut in suggested that he had seen a vision of someone murdering Nehemiah. Then, he suggested that the escape plan revealed to him was for Nehemiah and him to go to God's house, enter the temple and lock themselves inside. Seeking God's protection within God's own house; perhaps sounded reasonable. However, Nehemiah knew God would not tell him to do something that would be breaking the law.

When listening to the advisers along the way, always weigh the advice against the word of God. Often, many well-meaning Christians; outside of God's perfect will, do Satan's work for him. In this case, Nehemiah knew immediately that for he, a layman, to enter the temple was a sin. He would be breaking the Mosaic law were he to do so.

Realizing that truth, Nehemiah's eyes flew open wide and he realized this man proclaiming to be God's messenger had been hired by Sanballat. The enemy attacks had merely changed faces. To recognize this kind of attack, one must be versed in the truth of God's Words.

How to Be Victorious Over Enemy Attacks

1. Recognize the Enemy—always be aware that when you are doing God's work, Satan wants you defeated. Be always on guard to recognize his whispers, his lies, and his tactics. They seldom change much. He will try to cause you

to doubt God's call by making you feel unworthy. Therefore, he will disguise himself in many forms; trying to humiliate you. Whatever method possible, he wants you to sit down and stop doing God's work.

2. Pray—your only true source of victory is God. Cry out to Him, even if, yours is a desperate cry. It's not like God doesn't already know your doubts or trembling faith. However, He is waiting for you to acknowledge them and lay them at His feet. Part of your healing process is seeing and acknowledging your areas of weakness. Step by Step, one tiny bit at a time; God is always about the work of perfecting your heart, so that, you might have the greatest joy, hope and peace in Him.

3. Study God's Word: How can you recognize the lies, when the enemy attacks; if you don't know the truth?

4. Never forget, the victory is already won. God is much bigger than our enemy and has crushed Satan under His foot—one day, God will reign in perfect righteousness over a new heaven and a new earth. So, don't stop marching forward; even when you can't see through the clouds surrounding you.

5. Yes, sometimes it is good to pause, look up to God to ascertain you are following His plan and haven't strayed into doing your own will instead. However, do not stop in defeat when the enemy attacks; merely pause, ask for guidance and keep working. God will complete the work He has planned, His way and on His timing which is always perfect.

I Corinthians 15:57-58

But thanks be to God, which giveth us the victory through our Lord Jesus Christ. Therefore, my beloved brethren, be ye stedfast, unmoveable, always abounding in the work of the Lord, forasmuch as ye know that your labour is not in vain in the Lord.

Effie Darlene Barba

Chapter 12

Infrastructure

Despite all the opposition, the wall with its gates was finished. The opposition were depressed and defeated. Note, in referring to the other nations, Nehemiah reported they were *"much cast down in their own eyes: for they perceived that this work was wrought of our God"* (Nehemiah 6:16).

Our labors are not in vain; even when the going gets very tough, we must remember God is our strength and the victory is His. The wall was complete; but, there were other tasks that still lay ahead for the nation. Nehemiah named his brother Hanani as governor over Jerusalem; because *"he was a faithful man, and feared God"* (Nehemiah 7:2).

Now that the wall was built, there were many things to be done; because, the infrastructure would need to be addressed next. *"the city was large and spacious: but, the people in it were few, and the houses were not rebuilt"* (Nehemiah 7:4 NKJV).

Before moving forward, Nehemiah did four important things; because, he knew just having the wall would not keep the people safe without rules and regulations as to guarding them. The people needed an infrastructure built upon rules and regulations established by God, to protect them from heresy.

Ever since King Solomon's inclusion of so many ideologies, the nation had waxed and waned in their worship of God. This happened because he brought in so many people from other nations. He allowed them to build idolatrous altars to other gods and to teach their children to worship these false Gods. When so many foreigners did not truly embrace the ideals of Israel, the nation became a melting pot of ideas that turned them away from worshipping the true God. No longer was there any national pride; rather, divisions arose which led to their being taken captive. There loss of strength and position had begun within; by having so many who did not love the nation nor it's ideas.

REBUILDING THE INFRASTRUCTURE OF ORDER

Nehemiah, first placed a governor over the province; a faithful man who revered the Lord. Second, he established rules regarding the wall and the gates. *"And I said unto them, 'Let not the gates of Jerusalem be opened until the sun be hot; and while they stand by, let them shut the doors, and bar them: and appoint watches of the inhabitants of Jerusalem, everyone in his watch, and everyone to be over against his house'* (Nehemiah 7:3). Then, Nehemiah established Law officers and guards to protect the people.

To protect all the people, the gates remained closed and barred through the night. The gates opened during the day light, according to strict rules and regulations. People entering the city stopped at the gates. They had to be vetted before entering the city; so as, to prevent terrorist from entering to cause harm.

Third, he registered the people. *"And my put into mine heart to gather together the nobles, and the rulers, and the people that they might be reckoned by genealogy"* (Nehemiah 7:5). It was important to establish a registry to ascertain the people who were there; were so, legally. There were some who sought to be registered; however, they were claiming rights, despite being illegally there. Some were even among the priests. *"These sought their listing among those who were registered by genealogy, but it was not found; therefore, they were excluded from the priesthood as defiled"* (Nehemiah 7:64 NKJV).

Their exclusion was not a point of cruelty; but, rather necessary to protect the people from harm. These people seeking to be registered as priests to teach the people did not love God nor His laws. How could those who hated the nation and all they stood for be allowed to teach?

Then, all the people gathered their money to develop a plan of Rebuilding the infrastructure of their land. The houses, the streets, and the water systems had to be rebuilt.

REBUILDING AN INFRASTRUCTURE OF FAITH

"Ezra the priest brought the law before the congregation both of men and women, and all that could hear with understanding" (Nehemiah 8:2). All 42,360 people were gathered to listen as Ezra opened the books of the law to the people.

He began with a word of praise to God, and as he opened God's word, *"all the people, stood up; And Ezra blessed the Lord, the great God. And all the people answered, Amen, Amen with lifting up their hands: and they bowed their heads, and worshiped the Lord with their faces to the ground"* (Nehemiah 8:6). Imagine the scene! Everyone standing before God with their arms lifted high and their heads bowed low in worship.

As they stood there Ezra began to read to them the law. Suddenly, overwhelmed; they all began to weep. Each one felt the conviction of their own sins, their guilt and their shame. Then Nehemiah, Ezra and the Levites teaching said unto the people, *"this day is holy unto your Lord your God; mourn not, nor weep...Then he said unto them, Go your way, eat the fat, and drink the sweet, and send portions unto them for whom nothing is prepared: for this day is holy unto our Lord: neither be ye sorry: for the joy of the Lord is your strength"* (Nehemiah 8:9-10).

Note the charity. Establishing borders, building the wall, setting themselves apart in registering, and worshipping God provided them the ability to be generous and help others in the world. Until they stood firm as a nation, they had not the ability to really be charitable. Not allowing the others in, protecting their own sovereignty as a nation; that they could do the greater good through strength; united, one nation under God.

> *Establishing borders, building the wall, setting themselves apart in registering, and worshipping God provided them the ability to be generous and help others in the world.*

Chapter 13

The Importance of History and Ceremony

During the reading of the law, they came to a passage in the scripture referring to an important ceremony called the feast of the tabernacles. This feast was an important reminder of their history as a nation. It began on the 15th day of the seventh month and was to last for seven full days. During those seven days, they were to live in booths and to praise God for the harvest. This ceremony had been neglected by the children of Israel for many years. Remarkably, they read this portion of the law on the 2nd day of the seventh month. God always has perfect timing in all that He does.

Suddenly, they stopped everything to gather all the fruits of the land and to build the booths. They realized the importance of reestablishing ceremonies, remembering their history, and praising God. He had kept His covenant throughout the years, regardless of all their own failures as a nation to keep their covenant with Him. It was a reminder that God *"made the children of Israel to dwell in booths, when (He) brought them out of the land of Egypt"* (Leviticus 23:43). A reminder of God's promise, *"I am the Lord your God"* (Leviticus 23:43).

God remains in control of every detail of our lives.

It was no coincidence that they reached this passage just in time to prepare for the feast of the tabernacle; because, God knew the importance of His people remembering their true history. Ceremonies were important to help them recall all He had done; His faithfulness throughout the ages.

THE CEREMONY: A CELEBRATION OF HISTORY

So, the people went forth, and brought them (olive branches, pine branches, myrtle branches, palm branches, and branches of thick trees) and made themselves booths, everyone upon the roof of his house, and in their courts, and in the courts of the house of God, and in the street of the water gate, and in the street of the gates of Ephraim.

And all the congregations of them that were come again out of the captivity made booths, and sat under the booths: for since the days of Jeshua (Joshua) the son of Nun unto that day had not the children of Israel done so. And there was very great gladness.

Also, day by day, from the first day unto the last day, he read in the book of the law of God. And they kept the feast seven days; and on the eighth day was a solemn assembly, according unto the manner (Nehemiah 8:16-18).

Then, after all the ceremony was completed; on the 24th day of the seventh month, they all gathered with fasting, wearing sackclothes; with earth upon them. *"The seed of Israel separated themselves from all strangers, and stood and confessed their sins, and the iniquities of their fathers"* (Nehemiah 9:2). Confession of their sins was not a matter of international concern. The ceremony, the recollection of their history; was a matter of national concern. Returning to a sense of nationalism they knew was absolutely essential to secure their future as a nation under God.

PRAYER BEGINS WITH PRAISE

All the celebration had ended with a national prayer of repentance. Then, the priests and the Levites lead the nation in a four-part prayer. The prayer began with praise to God for who He is and all He had done.

> *"Stand up and bless the Lord your God*
>
> *for ever and ever: and blessed be thy*
>
> *glorious name, which is exalted above*
>
> *all blessing and praise. Thou, even*
>
> *thou, art Lord alone; thou hast made*
>
> *heave, the heaven of heavens, with all*
>
> *their host, the earth, and all things that*
>
> *are therein, the seas, and all that is*
>
> *therein, and thou preservest them all;*
>
> *and the host of heaven worshipeth thee.*

Thou art the Lord, The God" (Nehemiah 9: 5-7).

Prayer begins with acknowledging the one to whom we pray. Unless I remember to whom I am praying; my prayers seem very small. It is important that I remember: "God IS and He rewards those who diligently seek Him" (paraphrase of Hebrews 11:6). This is foundational to our living lives of Abiding, Steadfast Joy, as I spent several chapters in my book of the same name writing about this truth. We must write this truth upon our hearts to have the faith necessary to face the trials that lay before us.

PRAYER PART 2: RECALLING HISTORY AND GOD'S GRACE

The second part of the prayer in Nehemiah 9:7-31 is an honest remembrance of history ending with a celebration of God's grace. *"Nevertheless, for thy great mercies' sake thou didst not utterly consume them, nor forsake them; for thou art a gracious and merciful God"* (Nehemiah 9:31).

We must look back with honesty and integrity, remembering all that God has done; despite our failures. It is only God's grace that I am where I am in life; because, I do not deserve the grace I have been given.

The same is true as our nation. We cannot whitewash our own failures; however, we must with honesty remember God's grace through it all. Our pledge of allegiance reminds us that our nation was built upon Godly principals as "one nation, under God, indivisible with liberty and justice for all."

Although, we may have stumbled along this path at times; our forefathers set forth a future ideology a blueprint for which to follow. As a people; because of God's grace, we moved forward to ultimately repent of our sins, abolish slavery and provide equal rights for women. This was the futuristic dream of the founding fathers. Although many want to abolish our history; we must remember it with honesty and integrity in order to remain a nation.

Although many want to forget the truth of history, Francis Scott Key wrote the national anthem; not as a supporter of slavery. Rather, he wrote it as a stand against the slavery of England. He was held, along with many others, as a prisoner and slave upon a British ship. He was a staunch abolitionist, fighting against slavery. His third verse stood in condemnation against all the slavery and imprisonment enacted by the British. But, alas, if we do not teach the truth of history; we will fail to be able to move forward.

PART THREE: A REPENTANT HEART

The prayer recorded in Nehemiah 9 then turns to a realization that all their trials as a nation came because of their own sins as a nation. We must see the truth within our own hearts; recognizing that, were it not for grace, we deserved only God's wrath. All that I have, is only due to grace. When I realize that truth, I cannot bemoan that which I do not have; rather, I must praise God for what I do have.

When I realize that all I have is only due to Grace; I cannot bemoan that which I do not have; rather I must praise God for what I do have.

PART FOUR: A COVENANT TO SERVE GOD

The prayer in Nehemiah ends with a covenant to God, written and sealed by all the leaders of the nation of Israel. This included all the priests as well as the political leaders of the nation.

Have you made a covenant with God, to follow Him, to obey His commands? God's covenant to us is certain. He is faithful. But what about us? Can you at least make a covenant to spend time in Bible study, worship and prayer? Write it down, sign it and place it securely in your Bible; then, keep it.

A FOUR-PART PRAYER

This four-part prayer is blueprint of how we should pray as well.

1. Praise God for who He IS

2. Recall the history of all He has done

3. Repentant for sins and doubt

4. Covenant with God to follow Him, wherever He may lead you.

We must not forget who God is, nor the truth of our own history before God. With repentant hearts, recognizing that all we have is due to His grace; we must covenant to worship Him every day of our life from this day forward for the rest of our lives.

Effie Darlene Barba

CHAPTER 14:

Taxes, Tithes and Immigration

The wall completed. The rules of law and order restored. Immigration rules established. A covenant to God signed and sealed. Now, for the government to work; the people were to be committed to taxes and tithes.

Of note, in Nehemiah 10, taxes were decreased; while tithes remained at 10%. The people were poor, having recently returned from exile. Remember earlier, a revolt had broken out due to this? That was covered in Chapter 9. There had been greed and abuse among the leaders of the nation, which had been dealt with. Now, there would be tax reform as well. The leaders had all signed the covenant to serve God.

"And the rest of the people...all who separated themselves from the pagan

people of the land in order to obey the Law of God...joined their leaders and bound themselves with an oath. They swore a curse on themselves if they failed to obey the Law of God as issued by His servant Moses. They solemnly promised to carefully follow all the commands, regulations, and decrees of the Lord our Lord" (Nehemiah 10:28-29 TLB).

A CONFIRMED IMMIGRATION POLICY

Part of the oath sworn was to remain separate. They swore not to marry or allow in people who did not agree with their own values and beliefs. God commanded them to remain separate from the ideologies that could bring harm. This was not some phobia; because, if you recall those who adopted their belief system had always been welcomed in, such as

Ruth who was in the lineage of Christ; as was Rahab, the converted prostitute of Jericho. (see Matthew 1:5). Rules of immigration were necessary to protect them by not allowing in those who would bring harm to their nation or would teach their children idolatry.

Additionally, they swore to not trade with the foreigners who sold goods on the Sabbath. They could buy on other days; however, there had to be trade agreements which would not violate or cause harm to the people. Buying and selling on the Sabbath had been forbidden by God for the Jewish Nation, under the law of Moses. This was to ascertain they set aside the Sabbath for worship only. Otherwise, without the printing press; the people could easily forget the statutes of God which guided their lives into fullness. They had no Bible to read from, no personal means of learning God's Words to guide their lives; apart from going to hear His Word.

TAXES

The taxes were set aside to keep the structure of the temple and all of its functions running smoothly. Due to their poverty, tax reform was enacted. Instead of paying a half shekel, they would now pay a third shekel. (Nehemiah 10:32). With great joy, they willingly accepted the taxes; knowing that it would be used for the purposes intended. This required honest fiscal management by those receiving the taxes; rather than, mismanagement due to greed and abuse as had occurred previously.

Taxes are necessary to run a Government, provide for military and police protection as well as to maintain order within. In the New Testament, the church has been commissioned to care for the poor and disabled within a land. In the Old Testament Law, part of the reason for allowing their fields to rest on the seventh year was that the poor could gather all the crops that God grew in their fields that year. Remember also, how Ruth gleaned the fields behind the harvesters of Boaz? They were to always leave behind some of the crops to provide for the poor; although, all able bodies were to go into the fields and work for that provision.

As Christians, we should willingly pay our taxes. We should also be engaged through elections and writing our congressmen with how those taxes are being utilized.

TITHES

Of course, when it comes to money; we are to give God the first fruits of our labor. This should minimally be 10%. Then, we trust God to provide. But this is only the beginning, we are to be generous and help others as well; as God provides and leads us to do. Cheating God of His part, never works out financially.

This is often an act of faith and commitment to place God first in our lives and all that we do.

CHAPTER 15

Honoring the Unknown Heroes

Within the nation, as also the church, there are many unknown servants. They are the janitors, the secretaries, the people who park cars, the police, and those without whom no nation, business or church can survive. Yet, their names are seldom remembered. They serve in menial positions for minimal compensation. Furthermore, they often sacrifice more than God's servants who rise to fame; but, they do not seek fame. They willingly perform their tasks with diligence, laying their hearts and even their lives on the line for us. Unknown servants of God are certainly not unknown to Him.

The wall was built, civil laws re-established including immigration reform, taxes, and tithes within Jerusalem. Now, Nehemiah had the people cast lots to determine who would reside in Jerusalem and who would go to the surrounding villages. Those going to the surrounding villages would be able to farm the land, have livestock, and live a life without the stress of the city. However, those who drew the "short-straw" would remain in the city. They would be tasked with being guards, cleaning the streets, maintaining the temple and the city. Laborers for the good of the people, who would most likely live lives without the abundance that those in the villages would have. They would have to rely on the others to provide their support.

NEHEMIAH 11:1-2

> *And the rulers of the people dwelt at Jerusalem: the rest of the people also cast lots, to bring one of ten to dwell in Jerusalem the holy city, and nine parts*

to dwell in other cities. And the people blessed all the men, that willingly offered themselves to dwell at Jerusalem.

Note, the people blessed all who willingly offered themselves to serve in these menial jobs with no personal glory. How often do we forget those who labor and sacrifice themselves for the good of the kingdom? What about the prayer warriors whose names we never hear? The unknown servants of God who quietly go about the tasks that God has called them to; despite, their having no proclamations of greatness nor wealth on this earth? Passionately driven by a heart of love for God, they perform the tasks God has called them too; regardless, of their lack of recognition on this earth.

If I were to list the tasks and positions they hold, I would go on forever. However, I wish to turn and acknowledge two groups serving our nation here in particular: the men and women who serve in the military and those who serve as law officers.

UNKNOWN SERVANTS: MILITARY

I am privileged every day to meet some of those who have served; because, I work as a nurse practitioner in the VA system. These men and women are each one very special. What a privilege it is to meet them, as each one enriches my life. Their stories, lives, and the depth of heart with which they love our country goes beyond anything that I might be able to write here.

Humbly, they endure pains, sorrows, and memories with a stoic strength; I cannot even describe. Yet, each one says, they would do it all again; because, that is who they are. Although, they may be unknown servants to most; they are heroes, each deserving a plaque of honor. How blessed I am by God, to meet these heroes.

UNKNOWN SERVANTS: LAW OFFICERS

Another group whom we fail to give the recognition they deserve are the law officers who everyday go out to protect us. Underpaid, understaffed; they go out to face evils that many of us have never seen. We often don't see the depth of evil they face; because, they are there protecting us from it. Despite this, they are constantly under attack by our modern-day media and by those who promote chaos and lawlessness. For that reason, I want to share with you this poem I wrote several years ago. A reminder of their sacrifices. Also, a reminder that they are mothers, fathers, daughters, and sons; who put it all on the line to protect the rest of us. They are the unknown servants who deserve our respect.

Not Tonight

Into the deepest darkest night

Where evil lurks-hid from his sight

An Officer goes-prepared to fight

With all His strength and all His might

Praying to God, not tonight

He gently pulls His children near

Their smiles can lift his heart with cheer

He kisses boo-boos wipes their tears

And as He leaves for work He hears

Daddy, don't go, not tonight

She kisses him, to work he goes

And all the time, too well she knows

That he must face such evil foes

Phone clutched tight, her eyes then close

Lord, don't let it ring, not tonight

A mother awakens to whisper a prayer

Protect my son from sin's dark lair

Your warrior of truth-just and fair

Endowed by you with virtues rare

He's yours to call, please not tonight

Forgotten and paid a pauper's wage

Media and public he must assuage

While calmly holding back the rage

When violent criminals do engage

Pleading to God, not tonight

These officers protecting you

They sacrifice more than you knew.

When will you value what they do?

Or even stop to say, "Thank You"?

Shame on you, if not tonight

CONCLUDING THOUGHTS

Let's take the time to thank all those who are the unknown servants by always giving them the respect and love they deserve. We should be every day praying for them. Whether it be the cashier in the store, the secretary at work, the people parking cars at church, the law officers, the preachers willing to teach every Sunday in the small churches in rural areas, the veterans, and those who are serving in our military. Each of us need to let them know, they are not unknown servants; because, we know their name and God knows their name.

Be willing and ready to remind them,
they are not unknown servants because
God knows their name

CHAPTER 16

Joy Dedicating the Wall

Now came the moment to dedicate the wall. What an enormous joyous celebration was planned and carried out! The exiled captives were restored to their land. Furthermore, their faith and dedication to God was restored. Order established in their land through just laws, tax reform, and immigration reform. Law officers and the military reestablished to guard and protect their citizens. The temple (church) once more held a place of honor, the choir of singers with their orchestra haled the worship. Once more they could stand proud as a nation, unashamedly; because, God was on their side.

The corruption within their government had been abolished and they could trust the leadership; because, of their covenant with God. All of this was symbolized in the wall that God had commanded Nehemiah to build.

Since the time of David, there had not been a joyous celebration of this magnitude. Their love for God and praise for all He had down could be heard throughout the lands. *"Also, that day they offered great sacrifices, and rejoiced: for God had made them rejoice with great joy: the wives also and the children rejoiced: so that the joy of Jerusalem was heard even afar off"* (Nehemiah 12:43).

JOYOUS CELEBRATION OF SONGS

"And both the singers and the porters kept the ward of their God, and the ward of the purification, according to the commandment of David, and of Solomon his son. For in the days of David and Asaph of old there were chief of the singers, and songs of praise and

thanksgiving unto God. And all Israel in the days of Zerubbabel, and in the days of Nehemiah, gave the portions of the singers and the porters, every day his portion: and they sanctified holy things unto the Levites; and the Levites sanctified them unto the children of Aaron" (Nehemiah 12:47).

Nothing can raise the spirit quite like praise and worship music. Our music is very important. For the children of Israel, their music was filled with history as well; reminders of where they came from and how God had brought them out by His grace. Never did they want to forget their history; because, it reminded them as a nation, of their own failures toward God, and how He brought them back into full fellowship with Him. If they forget their history; they would more likely repeat their failures again.

If we forget our history, we are more likely to repeat our mistakes again

Haven't we all done that. I know I am more likely to falter and sin; when, I forget my sins of the past and how easily they slipped into my heart. Oh, I don't mean to dwell on my past failures; but, to remain diligent to recognize the earliest whispers that could draw me aside.

Also, note the people knew the importance of having these singers and musicians, providing provision for them. Perhaps, we should consider that before disbanding our military bands and singers. They bring the spirit of patriotism back into focus in our hearts and spirits.

DEDICATE THE WALL

The wall stood as a symbol that they had been restored as a nation and that God would be their protector. It stood as a symbol to all the nations of the world; detouring them from attacking the city of Jerusalem and its surrounding villages. Precisely, why the celebration to dedicate the wall was such an enormous and joyous event. Once more they were a nation under God, protected, secured, with national pride, integrity, and faith. That was a lot.

Effie Darlene Barba

Chapter 17

When Corruption Returns

Nehemiah returned to serve King Artaxerxes as he had promised; however, after a time, he obtained *"leave of the king"* (Nehemiah 13:6). Despite their having the wall and all having covenanted to God that they would follow Him; when Nehemiah returned to Jerusalem, he found corruption, evil, and disobedience.

How did he deal with the corruption and evil? It certainly was not by being tolerant or merciful. He faced the corruption and evil head on. There were four major areas of corruption that he dealt with in this manner: political corruption, financial corruption, societal corruption and domestic corruption.

POLITICAL CORRUPTION

Tobiah had been one of the enemies who tried to prevent Nehemiah and the people from building the wall. Imagine his reaction when he returned and found out *"Eliashib, the priest having the oversight of the chamber of the house of God was allied unto Tobiah: and he had prepared for him a great chamber, where aforetime they laid the meat offerings, the frankincense, and the vessels, and the tithes of the corn, the new wine, and the oil which was commanded to be given to the Levites and the singers, and the porters; and the offerings of the priests"* (Nehemiah 13:4-5).

This was true political treason at its highest! So, what did Nehemiah do?

And I came to Jerusalem and understood of the evil that Eliashib did for Tobiah, in preparing him a chamber

*in the courts of the house of God. And it
grieved me sore: therefore, I cast forth
all the household stuff of Tobiah out of
the chamber. Then I commanded, and
they cleansed the chambers: and thither
brought I again the vessels of the house
of God, with the meat offering and the
frankincense* (Nehemiah 13:8-9).

Evil and corruption had to be dealt with head
on. There was no "political correctness", nor could
there be. Neither, was there any negotiations. Political
Corruption at its highest degree was dealt with
immediately. Nehemiah not only threw into the streets
all of Tobiah's possession; he had the room thoroughly
cleaned or fumigated.

FINANCIAL CORRUPTION

*"And I perceived that the portions of the
Levites had not been given them: for the*

Levites and the singers, that did the work, were fled everyone to his field. Then contended I with the rulers, and said 'Why is the house of God forsaken?' And I gathered them together, and set them in their place" (Nehemiah 13:10-11).

"Then brought all Judah the tithe of the corn and the new wine and the oil unto the treasuries. Then I made treasurers over the treasuries" (Nehemiah 13:12-13). He made certain that the new treasurers, those responsible for the fiscal budget were responsible, honest men. It was with great caution, he chose the men he did; *"for they were counted faithful, and the office was to distribute unto their brethren"* (Nehemiah 13:13).

SOCIETAL CORRUPTION

The law of God for the children of Israel had been clear. There was to be no working nor was there to be the buying or selling of goods on the sabbath. Then, the lawbreakers seemed bent on doing just that. So, Nehemiah once more, pulled together all the rulers. He commanded that the gates be kept closed on the Sabbath. Lawbreakers, foreign or domestic had no place in the city. Although, this could potentially prevent some law-abiding people's entrance into the city on the Sabbath, the closing of the gates was essential to keeping the lawless out.

Some staged protests; but, Nehemiah dealt with them as well. *"So, the merchants and sellers of all kind of ware lodged without Jerusalem once or twice. Then I testified against them, and said unto them, Why lodge ye about the wall? If ye do so again, I will lay hands on you. From that time forth came they no more on the sabbath"* (Nehemiah 13:20-21).

In other words, "Go away, or I will lock you up!"

DOMESTIC CORRUPTION

Despite the people having made a covenant with God earlier not to intermarry with the pagan women, when Nehemiah returned; he found that they had broken this covenant. Not only had they married women from Ashdod, the Ammonites, and Moabite women; these women taught the children to not speak Hebrew. Instead they taught the children only their native language and to worship their pagan gods. Nehemiah rebuked them and asked God to curse them. Then, he plucked out the hair from the heads of those who broke the law. He did not shave their heads, he pulled their hair until they were bald.

"And their children spake half in the speech of Ashdod, and could not speak in the Jew's language, but according to the language of each people" (Nehemiah 13:24).

Why was it so important they learn the language? The children could never understand the history of the nation of Israel; unless they knew the language. They would never worship God, nor would they grow up with the same ideals of the nation. Instead, they would bring pagan worship into the country. God had set the rules to protect the nation from heresy, not to be cruel or racist. This, as I previously pointed out, was proven in previous scripture where Rahab and Ruth were fully accepted into the nation; because, they embraced the ideas and the worship of the nation. In fact, both women were in the lineage of Jesus Christ as shown in the gospel of Matthew. So, this was a big deal; if the children did not know the language, they certainly would not embrace the Jewish nation. Jesus reached out His ministry to all who would believe and embrace the gospel message.

HOW DID HE DEAL WITH CORRUPTION?

So, what did Nehemiah do? He went straight to the men who had married these women and allowed their pagan ideologies and worship to take hold in the society.

> *"And I contended with them and cursed them, and smote certain of them, and plucked off their hair, and made them swear by God, saying, "Ye shall not give your daughters unto their sons, nor take their daughters unto your sons, or for yourselves"* (Nehemiah 13:26).

Then he reminded them of their history. After all, what began the fall of the nation; leading to their division into two nations, weakening them so they were taken captive, had been King Solomon bringing so many pagan wives into the nation and allowing them to set up shrines to idols.

> *"Did not Solomon king of Israel sin by these things? Yet among many nations was there no king like him, who was beloved of his God, and God made him king over all Israel: nevertheless, even him did outlandish women cause to sin. Shall we then hearken unto you to do all this great evil, to transgress against our God in marrying strange wives?* (Nehemiah 13:26-27).

But, Nehemiah didn't stop there.

> *"And one of the sons of Joiada, the son of Eliashib the high priest, was son-in-law to Sanballat the Horonite: therefore, I*

chased him from me" (Nehemiah 13:28). They had brought evil in through the front door. Then Nehemiah said, "Thus cleansed I them from strangers, and appointed wards of the priests and the Levites, everyone in his business; and for the wood offering at times appointed, and for the first fruits. Remember me, O my God, for good (Nehemiah 13:31).

HOW SHOULD WE DEAL WITH CORRUPTION IN OUR OWN LIVES?

Pluck it out! Cleanse the areas where it stood. Our battle against corruption within our own hearts or the evil hidden within, displaying itself as jealousy, anger, selfishness, doubt or despair remains that: a battle! Yet, that battle was won for us on the cross. We do not stand alone to overcome; instead, we are promised victory in Jesus Christ, our Savior and Lord.

When Nehemiah prayed, *"Remember me, O my God, for good"* (Nehemiah 5:19, 6:14, 13:22,29, and 31); it wasn't a prayer for God to remember him. It was a "plea for help, not merely a request that God not forget something. Judah's leader did not want his efforts of reform to be undone by the people's neglect."[26] (Getz 2004)

We should each ask that same prayer, "God, remember me for good. Don't let me neglect your word, your covenant and your laws in my life. I do not want to falter or fail in this mission of life you have given me, and I can't do it on my own without you."

How often does a teacher of the word, lose their testimony; because, they slip and fall? Let us each plea

---

[26] Getz, "Nehemiah", 695

to God that He "remember me and keep my foot from slipping."

Chapter 18

Why America Needs to Study Nehemiah

When you look down through the corridors of history, few nations have survived such oppressions, years of captivity and still stand. Yet, Israel stands as a nation with one of the highest life expectancies[27], highest standards of living within the middle east[28], and highest educated, with one of the largest numbers of men and women receiving tertiary degrees[29].

Nehemiah was a layman who played a large role in re-establishing social, political and financial order to the nation after a long period of exile. We can certainly learn much from the book of Nehemiah, if we wish to survive as a nation. Throughout, this in-depth study of

---

[27] Human Development Index and its components(Report). United Nations Development Programme. Accessed 12/20/17

[28] Ibid.

[29] Education at a Glance: Israel (Report). Organisation for Economic Co-operation and Development. 15 September 2016

Nehemiah, there appeared so many parallels to many of the issues faced by our nation today. Furthermore, there lays within the history leading up to Nehemiah's time even more parallels of what lead to their captivity and near decimation.

Although King Solomon began as a mighty king, bringing the nation of Israel into the forefront of all nations, with prosperity, power and peace with God as his guide. During that time period, they were admired throughout the surrounding lands. *"So, king Solomon exceeded all the kings of the earth for riches and for wisdom. And all the earth sought to Solomon to hear his wisdom, which God had put in his heart"* (I Kings 10:23-24).

Many nations desired to join in alliance with Israel and King Solomon married many foreign women to establish treaties; yet, he made a grave error. He did not vet these women's ideologies. So, they brought with them other ideologies as well as their pagan worship. Instead of his teaching them of God, they pulled him into their pagan worship; forsaking that which had made him great to begin with.

"For it came to pass...that his wives turned away his heart after other gods: and his heart was not perfect with the Lord his God" (I Kings 11:4).

FORGETTING WHAT MADE THEM GREAT

As a result of Solomon's grave error, the nation split into two; after his death. This occurred in 931 B.C. "The 10 Northern tribes were initially ruled by Jeroboam, and the Southern tribes (Judah and Benjamin) were ruled by Rehoboam."[30] (Getz 2004). No longer was there the national pride that glued them together as a nation. Nor was there the faith that bound them together as a nation. All their original

---

[30] Getz, "Nehemiah", 673

foundations, that which made them great; were cast aside. Battles and fighting from within, made them an easy target. Furthermore, all the diversity of ideas brought in and taught by Solomon's wives to the children; caused them to forsake the truths interwoven into the fabric of their strength. Forsaking the history which made them great, they now were destined to repeat all the errors of their forefathers.

"Both kingdoms, however, continued to be characterized by idolatry and immorality. And as God had forewarned, His hand of judgment fell on all of Israel because of their sin. The Northern Kingdom fell first, and the people were taken into captivity by the Assyrians in 722 B.C. The Babylonians brought about the fall of the Southern Kingdom in 586 B.C."[31] (Getz 2004).

---

[31] Getz, "Nehemiah", 673

Yet, just as God had prophesied through Isaiah, Jeremiah, Habakkuk and Zephaniah; God remained faithful to His covenant, despite the people. There would be a remnant of faithful Jews who would be brought back to Judea to rebuild the nation. Daniel was one of the faithful, whose prayers came to fruition.[32] His faith and courage transformed the heart of the pagan King who had taken him captive: King Nebuchadnezzar, allowing for the survival of the children of Israel. Esther stood in the gap protecting her people, risking her own life as Queen; during those years of captivity.

God had a plan of good for His people, and He paved the way for all who would listen. Just as He promised in Jeremiah 29: 11-14.

---

[32] For more information regarding Daniel, I did a full series in 2016 beginning with
https://www.myglorytoglory.com/christianblog/how-to-find-purpose-and-joy-in-this-world.html

For I know the thoughts that I think toward you, saith the Lord, thought of peace, and not of evil, to give you an expected end. Then shall ye call upon me, and ye shall go and pray unto me, and I will hearken unto you. And ye shall seek me, and find me, when ye shall search for me with all your heart. And I will be found of you, saith the Lord: and I will turn away your captivity, and I will gather you from all the nations, and from all the places whither I have driven you, saith the Lord; and I will bring you again into the place when I cause you to be carried away captive (Jeremiah 29:11-14).

Are we seeking and searching for Him with all our Heart?

ZERUBBABEL, EZRA, AND NEHEMIAH

When Cyrus of Persia overtook the Babylonian empire, he was amazed that God had spoken of him in the book of Jeremiah, long before he was born.

Now in the first year of Cyrus king of Persia, that the word of the Lord spoken by the mouth of Jeremiah might be accomplished, the Lord stirred up the spirit of Cyrus king of Persia, that he made a proclamation throughout all his kingdom, and put it also in writing, saying, "Thus saith Cyrus king of Persia, All the kingdoms of the earth hath the Lord God of heaven given me; and he hath charged me to build him an house in Jerusalem, which is in Judah. Who is there among you of all his people? The

Lord his God be with him, and let him go

up (2Chronicles 36:22-23).

The first group of exiles returning to their land was led by Zerubbabel in 538 B.C. "Over a period of years and tremendous opposition from the Samaritans, the returnees eventually succeeded in rebuilding the temple in 515 B.C. In 458 B. C. a second group, led by Ezra the priest returned. Ezra began to re-establish their faith; however, "they found the Jews in Israel in a state of spiritual and moral degradation."[33] (Getz 2004)

Then, God sent an unlikely person; Nehemiah, who brought about order, beginning with building the wall. Now, do you realize the importance of studying Nehemiah? God chooses sometimes the most unlikely

---

[33] Getz, "Nehemiah", 673

person to lead a nation. Yet, it is God who sets up the rulers of a nation.

Still, before we can rebuild this our nation; we must recognize the evil within which is tearing our nation apart, which is why I have decided to dedicate an entire section to address just that.

THE EVIL WITHIN

Effie Darlene Barba

Chapter 19:
Recognizing the Evil Within

Before confronting the evil within our nation, we must take a moment to reflect personally and as a nation to recognize the evil. Throughout the study of Nehemiah, we reflected upon the history of Israel. What happened? Why did they fall into captivity? What can we as a nation learn from them? They had allowed evil within, first dividing the nation through their own internal fighting. Quickly, the break from within led to their splintering into two, making them such an easy target for the other nations to destroy. They failed to acknowledge or confront the Evil within and that lead to their demise.

During the reign of King Solomon, the nation rose to a place of great power and wealth in the world. People from everywhere wanted to be a part of that great nation. King Solomon, in his peak of success, began to believe them invincible. Then, as an act of benevolence; he married women from many nations, expanding his power and influence. Perhaps, believing his own wisdom and greatness would prevail; he allowed them to continue to worship their pagan gods. Instead of standing firm, ultimately; they drew him into their false ideologies, rather than he making certain they learned from his.

It begins that way. The evil within grew; creating a divide that ended in the nation splitting into two. They turned their back on God. First the Northern Kingdom was taken captive and later the Southern Kingdom.

Yet, God remained faithful and drew once more the few who followed Him back to Jerusalem. Despite His faithfulness, the broken walls and the evil within once more could have destroyed them. Then, God sent Nehemiah to build the wall and to restore the nation.

THE EVIL WITHIN

During the late 1800s and throughout the 1900s, our nation thrived. As a nation built upon faith, Christian influence thrived. We divided once over slavery; yet, the nation was restored after a bitter civil war. Christian principles won. The Battle Hymn of the Republic stood as their theme song; that God's truth would march on. The writer of the lyrics, Julia Ward Howe went on to lead the women's suffrage movement.

As a nation under God, we made great strides; yet, once more we see a division rising from evil within. Christians led scientific research and indeed began the institutions of higher learning; believing that a personal God reveals Himself to mankind. Still, with the introduction of Darwin's Theory of Evolution; many scientists, desiring to remove God from the

185

picture adopted it as law. This began the naturalist scientific movement.

Despite the failure of any experiments, or even fossil imprints proving the theory; the theory was pronounced as though proven and began to be taught as law. Indeed, when the Big Bang Singularity theory was first introduced; the atheistic scientists tried to prove it wrong. Despite their efforts, proof after proof presented itself; proving that the earth began with one big bang (as already told us in Genesis 1).

At the same time, a philosophical movement called the secular humanists took hold. Their first manifesto written in 1933, set the stage. Presenting themselves as a progressive religious alternative; based on the natural inner goodness of mankind without the need of God or His restrictions, they grew in both political power and spread throughout the nation. They strongly believed they could transform all to a greater society by first overtaking the education of the children. Their ideals of sexual freedom and self-actualization drew widespread support.

A NEW AGE OF ENLIGHTMENT—THE OLD EVIL WITHIN

Wanting to believe that humans have evolved to a place of goodness, even the Christians embraced their ideals. This has led us to where we are as a nation-divided by ideals. Before we can confront the evil within, we must understand this ideology. Is it too late to confront it? That is a question we must ask ourselves. God is a gracious and loving God, who reaches out to each and every human. The question is: "will we listen?" Just as God restored Israel in Nehemiah's time, will He restore us as a nation? That depends on us.

God said, "*If my people, which are called by my name, shall humble themselves, and pray and seek my*

187

face, and turn from their wicked ways; then, will I hear from heaven and will forgive their sin, and will heal their land" (2 Chronicles 7:14).

Over the course of the next few chapters, I want to tell you more about the evil ideology within; and present to you an argument as to why the Christian worldview is superior. Only if we understand how we allowed this in and seek the truth of God's word, can we be restored both individually and as a nation. We need to learn from Nehemiah, how to be restored.

Concluding Thoughts

Before we can confront the evil within our nation, we must first confront the evil within our own hearts. God in His Grace, mercy and Love has provided a way of salvation for us through Jesus Christ, His son. Let us turn to Him. We must return to God's word.

Through prayer and Bible study, we can grow to become witnesses for Him.

We can become the light that shines into the darkness surrounding us; as we willingly surrender to Him. Never forsake your time alone with Him or your family devotions; because, all too quickly the evil grows within our own hearts. Never forget: *For God so loved the world that He gave His Only Begotten Son, that whosoever believeth in Him should not perish; but have everlasting life* (John 3:16).

It must begin with our addressing our own hearts, protecting our own family by teaching them the truth, and we must take the time to pray. Prayer is our greatest power, allowing God to control our thoughts and our actions. We cannot do this; if we the Christians within this nation leave our Bibles laying on the bedside table unopened.

189

We must remember that the evil we fight are not the individuals; rather, the ideologies. That must first begin with me. I must study to know what is true and then how to defend the truth of God to the world around me. We must teach our children how to defend their faith. Knowledge is essential. First, we must understand what it is we are confronting; and, then, we must learn how to take captive our own thoughts. Only then can we be the light of truth to the world.

For though we walk in the flesh, we do not war after the flesh: (For the weapons of our warfare are not carnal, but mighty through God to the pulling down of strong holds) Casting down imaginations, and every high thing that exalteth itself against the knowledge of God, and bringing into captivity every thought to the obedience of Christ; And having in a readiness to revenge all disobedience, when your obedience is fulfilled (2 Corinthians 10:3-6).

We must learn through diligently studying God's word as Paul instructed Timothy, *Study to shew thyself approved unto God, a workman that needeth not to be ashamed, rightly dividing the word of truth* (2 Timothy 2:15).

Always be ready to give an answer. *But sanctify the Lord God in your hearts: and be ready always to give an answer to every man that asketh you a reason of the hope that is in you with meekness and fear* (I Peter 3:15).

For that reason, I want to explain the secular humanist movement and how it moved us into the post-modernist think tank. Remember always that the ideology is what we are at battle with, not the individuals promoting it. Indeed, we must learn how to defend our faith; but, always mindful that we are doing so in order to spread the gospel message, even to those who so staunchly battle against us. Our desire is to bring the sinner to repentance; not to, hate the sinner, merely the sin. We must learn to see the sinner through the eyes of eternity. Always, remain mindful of your own sin, *that in the ages to come He might shew the exceeding riches of His grace in His kindness toward us through Christ Jesus. For by grace are ye saved through faith; and that not of yourselves: it is the gift of God: Not of works, lest any man should boast* (Ephesians 2:7-9).

So, let us study that we might learn how to defend our faith as individuals. And let us pray for our nation and the message of Christ Jesus to heal the wounds that divide us.

Chapter 20

Utopia Apart from God?

The Secular Humanist Movement and ideas invaded everything during the twentieth century. Believing that mankind had evolved beyond a need for God or religious institutions, they put their faith in humans and science to lead us into a perfect Utopia. Laying aside faith in God and the "restrictions" placed by religion, they believed that mankind evolved into creatures of greatness and kindness. They taught that Man could find self-actualization and Being apart from God.

Why were their ideals so quickly embraced and grew unchecked by even the Christians? Because mankind wanted to believe in their own individual greatness, their ideas were embraced and as a society we sought after this Utopia they promised. It was the same lie whispered to Adam and Eve so long ago; but, it came in a new package with great promotional advertisements.

After all, it was what the human heart wanted to hear. With Darwin's Theory of Evolution, suddenly they held fast to the ideas that we were an evolved society which could through experimentation, science, and new ideals find Utopia without God. If we laid aside our beliefs in God, they said we could further discover our own Utopia in the here and now. With philosophers such as Karl Marx leading the crusade, we could become a society that truly lived in a Utopia on this planet called earth. What are their Core Beliefs? Well, I shall let their own words answer that question.

CORE BELIEFS OF SECULAR HUMANISM

Secular humanism is a philosophical worldview proclaiming that through scientific discovery, experimentation, and the "freedom" of human thought; humanity, apart from supernatural ideologies (a belief in God), can achieve "happiness, self-realization, joyful exuberance, creative endeavors and excellence, the actualization of the good life— not only for the individual but for the greater community"[34] (Kurtz 2010) in the here and now.

Established officially as a worldview in 1933 with the Humanist Manifesto I; they trace their ideals "to the philosophers, scientists, and poets of classical Greece and Rome.[35]" (Kurtz 1980) Since then, some ideals evolved over time, leading to later Manifestos. However, there were some core beliefs that remained constant, which are as outlined on the following pages. Remember, I am letting their own words speak for them as to what they believe.

---

[34] Paul Kurtz, *Multi-secularism: A New Agenda,* (New Brunswick, NJ: Transaction, 2010), 3
[35] Paul Kurtz, *A Secular Humanist Declaration,* (Amherst, NY: Prometheus Books, 1980), 14

What is Most Important to the Secular Humanist?

For the secular humanist, "Man is not only that which he conceives himself to be, but that which he wills himself to be, ... man is nothing other than what he makes of himself."[36] (Sartre 2007) Furthermore, the secular humanist believes that "religion has blighted people's lives, imposing restrictions and inhibitions in the name of divine commands which thwart people's aspirations to happiness."[37] (Norman 2012) Only through freedom and self-reflection, can one hope to find a deeper meaning to life; unchained, by religious dogma. *Or so they think.*

---

[36] Jean Paul Sartre, *Existentialism is a Humanism,* Trans. Carol Macomber, (New Haven and London: Yale University Press, 2007), 22

[37] Richard Norman, *On Humanism,* 2nd ed. (London: Taylor and Francis, 2012), 16.

However, with this, they believe, comes a responsibility to all of humanity. Paul Kurtz wrote: "each person is responsible for his or her own future and that of society... improving the lives of everyone on the planet as far as we are capable of doing."[38] (Kurtz 2010) Sartre writes, "man is condemned to be free;" (Sartre 2007)[39] because, without God or a sin nature to blame, humans are "left alone without excuse.... responsible for everything he does." (Sartre 2007)[40] The future of all of humanity, the earth and the planetary system's survival rests upon the shoulders of each human born. *I thought they said without restrictions?*

---

[38] Paul Kurtz, *Multi-secularism: A New Agenda.* (New Brunswick, NJ: Transaction, 2010), 237

[39] Jean Paul Sartre, *Existentialism is a Humanism,* Trans. Carol Macomber, (New Haven and London: Yale University Press, 2007), 29.

[40] Ibid.

Epistemology of Secular Humanists

The secular humanists believe that we must place science above all else to learn who we are. Placing Scientific Observation, experimentation, and rational analysis as their ultimate source; secular humanists believe "human beings ... need to use intelligence and goodwill to solve problems... to negotiate differences rationally and to work out compromises using science, reason, and humanist values"[41] (Kurtz 2010) As "part of a vast cosmic scene, a magnificent awe-inspiring universe that we can unravel and comprehend—we need to continue to use our critical intelligence to explore and explain the cosmos: the polarity of chance and contingency, regularity and order, chaos and plurality."[42] (Kurtz 2010)

---

[41] Paul Kurtz, *Multi-secularism: A New Agenda.* (New Brunswick, NJ: Transaction, 2010) 234.
[42] Ibid., 256

Yet, skepticism must remain at the forefront of this process. "we need some skepticism about even the reaches of science or the possibilities it provides for reforming our moral life, let alone the pitfalls of religion or ontology or ideology."[43] (Kurtz 1985) Skepticism "is both the beginning and the end of wisdom...It is a corrective, an antidote to the morally intoxicated of every age."[44] (Kurtz 1985)

Source and Nature of Morality

Paul Kurtz in his debate with William Lane Craig presented the core elements of what the secular humanist believes concerning goodness as follows. "Morality and moral behavior do not depend on divine commandments but on the development of an internal moral sense and, particularly in the young, the growth of moral character, and the capacity for moral

---

[43] Paul Kurtz, "Moral Faith and Ethical Skepticism Reconsidered", *The Journal of Value Inquiry* 19, (January 1, 1985), 65
[44] Ibid

reasoning."[45] (Kurtz 2009) The Humanist Manifesto III declares that humans are an integral part of nature, the result of unguided evolutionary change. (*Then how exactly did we develop reasoning, or even the idea of good or evil?*)

Almost all secular humanists believe in utilitarism. "The creed which accepts as the foundation of morals, Utility, or the Greatest Happiness Principle, holds that actions are right in proportion as they tend to promote happiness, wrong as they tend to produce the reverse of happiness."[46] (Mill 1998) (*The question I have is "whose happiness are we talking about?)*

Secondly, they say they believe in objective morality which for them is the belief that there are

---

[45] Paul Kurtz, "The Kurtz/Craig Debate: Is Goodness without God Good Enough?", *Is Goodness Without God Good Enough?: A Debate on Faith, Secularism, and Ethic,* (Lanham, MD: Rowman & Littlefield Publishers, 2009), 25

[46] John Stuart Mill and Roger Crisp, *Utilitarianism,* (Oxford: Oxford University Press, 1998), 55

things within the universe itself which present a moral code of allowing one to know what is right or wrong. As Paul Kurtz debated, "There is an evolution within human history and civilization and a corresponding development of basic moral principles, and these are often won only after arduous struggles, as in the battles against slavery and racism and for the rights of women."[47] (Kurtz 2009) (*Somehow, they failed to remember that it was the Christians who led these battles, not the atheists.*)

Beliefs Held Tightly

Among the ideals held dearest to the Secular Humanist, as noted in their Second Manifesto, were the belief in sexual freedom, divorce, abortion, assisted suicide and euthanasia. They believed Utopia could be found through infiltrating our school systems, teaching our young, taking over the news medias, and

---

[47] Kurtz, "Goodness without God", 35

overtaking our political arena. Within the next chapter, we will look further at what went wrong, how they adjusted their ideas to move forward, and how they won the battles even in the Supreme Court. Their ideals, though flawed; promised mankind a way of being "like God" individually; however, their experiments failed and now we face a society where truth is relative, and the violence of nihilism has split our nation in two.

CONCLUDING THOUGHTS

We as Americans allowed these ideas to infiltrate the core of our own belief systems with such ease; because, much like Adam and Eve, we wanted to believe that we are good and that we could be god. Although, as God pointed out, *"the imagination of man's heart is evil from his youth"* (Genesis 8:21). Without God's intervening hand of Grace, there would be no good (an argument I will more fully develop as we move forward in this book).

Jesus provides a way for our hearts to be transformed through faith in Him and the ongoing work of the Holy Spirit, here and now. He conquered death and sin to rise victoriously. One day He will return. The Utopia our heart so longs for, will be the eternity we live in His presence one day.

Effie Darlene Barba

Chapter 21

When the Experiments All Failed

Throughout the twentieth century, we were bombarded with the new ideals presented by the secular humanist movement. Abraham Maslow presented his hierarchy of needs for every man and woman to reach full self-actualization; although, he believed less than 3% achieve this goal. Still, he laid forth a foundation or goal that we might structure society is some manner that all men would become benevolent and kind. Although, sad to say; it never worked, despite our best efforts. Indeed, we became more self-absorbed and ego centrical than ever.

There were many other psychologists and philosophers at the same time, such as Jean Paul Sartre, Friedrich Nietzsche, Sigmund Freud, and Karl Marx. All believed that man, without God; could be capable of being loving, kind, and fully self-actualizing in a society filled with happiness, joy, benevolence and hope. Based on science, experimentation, and reasoning; humanity would flourish into a global utopian world. So, what happened? When the social experiments all failed, did they abandon their ideals? No, in fact they doubled down.

Hitler's atrocious acts against the Jewish people were grounded in scientific "survival of the fittest." As David Berlinski pointed out in *The Devil's Delusion,* "A sinister current of influence ran from Darwin's Theory to Hitler's policy of extermination."[48] (Berlinski 2009) The biological scientists believed that annihilation of these non-integrating God-fearing people would be better for society as a whole. (*Hmm, sounds like what*

---

[48] David Berlinski, *The Devil's Delusion,* (New York: Basic Books, 2009), 27.

the secular humanists are saying about Christians today?)

Stalin relied heavily on the ideals of Karl Marx (one of the earliest secular humanist philosophers), leading the USSR into the future from a group of peasant farmers into the industrial revolution, while killing all who stood in his way. After all, if there is no God; who, can say anything is wrong? Did not both Adolf Hitler, along with the German People believe this to be for the good of society? Or Stalin who believed he was leading the USSR into greatness; where they would flourish? Yet, despite these failures; the secular humanists regrouped to write Manifesto II in 1973. Instead of accepting the failure of their own ideals; because, experimentation had proven them wrong; they merely rewrote their ideals hoping to try again with the same old ideas. *(Isn't that the definition of a fool, believing that you can do the same old thing and hope for a different outcome?)*

BASED ON SCIENCE OR NOT?

Everything that the secular humanists base their core beliefs upon, according to them is science and scientific experimentation. So, when socialism and Nazism failed; they had to come back to say in Manifesto II, "Nazism has shown the depths of brutality of which humanity is capable. Other totalitarian regimes have brought evil as well as good. Science has sometimes brought evil as well as good."[49] Despite this they dug deeper in to a belief that "religion was the greater evil" in part as Christopher Hitchens and Charles Dawkins proclaimed because of the dangerous sexual repressions. Perhaps, that is why

---

[49] Humanist Manifesto II, 1973 by the American Humanist Association,

Humanist Manifest II dealt a lot with sexual freedoms, promotion of abortion and divorce. But how did that work out?

With so many buying into these ideologies, we have an epidemic of suicide, single parent homes facing poverty, and drug addiction because people are seeking personal happiness where none can be found. Marriage became about "what can you do to fulfill my desires for happiness?" If you cannot, then I will try someone else. Counterfeit joys of sexual freedoms, alcohol, and drugs cannot fulfill the true longings found within the heart of mankind. So, many are left with the feelings of loneliness, brokenness, and despair. Again, a social experiment that failed; yet, that did not detour the secular humanist from marching onward.

Furthermore, when the scientists discovered "the Big Bang"; many tried to hide its discovery, because, it gave credence to the Universe having had a beginning. Something, which the secular humanists did not want to hear. Until then, they believed the Universe to have been eternally present, they had placed all their faith in this! With the Big Bang Singularity Theory; well, that just did not fit in. As more and more evidence proved the case; they were forced to accept it, reluctantly. Proudly, they proclaimed that science will one day discover the "cause" of the Big Bang. Yet, whatever it is must be outside time (Eternal), outside space (omnipresent), and outside of energy/matter (omnipotent).

The question then rises: "Do the Secular Humanists really believe that science can lead the way; or only when science fits their mold?" Indeed, the atheistic bias seen within the scientific community at large; has crept into the experiments themselves. Evolution has failed to be proven; although, scientist have tried desperately to prove it to be the case. All the experiments and even archeological finds prove it false. Still, they cling desperately to evolution as though a law; while, calling the "The Big Bang Singularity" truth a theory.

So, What Did They Do Next?

In 1980, "*A Secular Humanist Declaration*" was presented in the humanist magazine "Free Inquiry" written by Paul Kurtz. In it he calls for a democratic secular humanist movement. He also denounced all religious institutions as being invasively disallowing of freedom of thought or inquiry; demanding tolerance. *That is unless you are Christian.* Then in 2000, the

Humanist Manifesto III; called for a planetary humanism. *Having failed in each arena to achieve the Utopian society; it would only be reasonable to make it global?* Yet, that is what Paul Kurtz proposed:

Humanist Manifesto 2000 emphasizes that we are responsible for our own destiny, and that we can best solve our problems by rational inquiry. It provides a strong defense of human rights. Of special significance is the "Planetary Bill of Rights and Responsibilities": we have a responsibility to humanity as a whole, to end poverty and disease, and to ensure peace and prosperity for every member of the world community. The Manifesto recommends concrete reforms to achieve these goals: a new planetary income tax, the regulation of global conglomerates, open access to the media, populations stability, environmental protection, an effective security system, development of World Law, and a new World Parliament.[50] (Kurtz 1999)

Let's look at where it has lead the United States; even to the dismay of the secular humanists. Our schools and campuses have reached the place of intellectual, scientific, and historic relativism in which truth is whatever I believe it to be. In other words, there is no truth; unless of course you disagree with their alternate reality, then, you are definitely wrong.

But why are the secular humanists surprised by this shift to post-modernist's relativism. After all, they

---

[50] Kurtz, Paul, "The Promise of Manifesto 2000", *Free Inquiry,* Winter 1999, 5

themselves ignored the scientific evidence when it did not fit their narrative. Furthermore, without God; who defines good or evil? With self-actualization and self-preservation as one's goal; how can utilitarianism ever be about self-sacrifice for another's happiness over one's own?

FACING THE LIES, FINDING TRUTH

Before we can face the evil within; we each must stop and look at how we arrived in this place to begin with. Gradually, we embraced the ideologies of the secular humanist movement and gave them the power to overtake our thought systems; making us question God. They infiltrated our political system, our laws, and our schools. Suddenly, we felt guilty for our faith in Jesus Christ. We apologized to our children, our neighbors, and our Christian friends for our beliefs. It is no wonder we have reached this place in history. So, what can we do? Over the next few chapters, I want to expose the fallacies of the Secular Humanistic Worldview and present for you a case for Christianity. Only after we grasp the truth, can we confront the future. Knowledge is key.

Only the Bible presents for us the truth of the human condition and a means of salvation. Only in Christ Jesus can we find our true identity; abounding with true hope, joy, love and strength. Created in the image of God; our hearts long for royalty, righteousness, and the life we were created for. Yet, free will allows us to choose; and mankind repeatedly chooses self-promotion and self-reliance. Which is why we in general remain so restless, disenchanted, unsatisfied, and in general, miserable human beings; unless, we turn to Jesus Christ. The Bible reveals the reality of mankind's dilemma. We need to be born again as a new creature in Christ Jesus; so, that we might fulfill the destiny originally planned by God for the human race.

Therefore, if any man be in Christ, he is a new creature: old things are passed away; behold, all things are become new. And all things are of God, who hath reconciled us to himself by Jesus Christ, and hath given to us the ministry of reconciliation; To wit, that God was in Christ, reconciling the world unto himself, not imputing their trespasses unto them; and that committed unto us the word of reconciliation. Now then we are ambassadors for Christ, as though God did beseech you by us: we pray you in Christ's stead, be ye reconciled to God.

For he hath made him to be sin for us,

who knew no sin; that we might be made

the righteousness of God in Him (2

Corinthians 5:17-21).

CONCLUSION:

All the social experiments of the secular humanists have failed to bring peace. They failed in Germany, in the Socialist regime of Stalin, and they have lead us to a place of division, anger and relativism in the United States. Christians allowed these false ideologies in and allowed them to gain great power; because, deep down we wanted to believe in our own "goodness without God." Yet, without God, where is there any foundation for "good?" Relativism, militant atheism, a desire for socialism, and nihilism plagues our youth. Is it too late for our country? I don't think so; God's promises have always remained true and His promise to Israel was:

> *If my people, which are called by my name, shall humble themselves, and pray, and seek my face, and turn from their wicked ways; then will I hear from heaven, and will forgive their sin, and will heal their land* (2 Chronicles 7:14).

That same promise is to us today. More recently, we have seen hope for our nation returning to God; but, we cannot become complacent, and we must learn from Nehemiah what true restoration looks like: spiritual, political, and social.

Chapter 22

Secular Humanism Fails as a Worldview

For any worldview to stand as true, there are basic criteria it must meet. Yet, despite its proclamations of being based on scientific evidence; the secular humanist movement continued to expand, grow and engulf much of modern thought without any of their experiments working. To begin with, they laid forth in Humanist Manifest I what is considered an open door to radical ad hoc readjustment. That is, if any part fails; they could just rewrite that portion and still claim the rest as true, despite its inconsistencies. The first two sentences were just that, "The Manifesto is a product of many minds. It was designed to represent a developing point of view, not a new creed."[51] Despite this statement, they held fast to most

---

[51] Humanist Manifesto I, 1933

of their developing points of view as though they were written in stone as truth.

Untested, the ideas were no more than the developing thought of some men. Perhaps like a social theory, they again held fast to "man is what he makes himself to be." While they could find no basis for mankind being innately good, desiring to be truthful, loving and kind: that remained a part of their mantra. How did evolution bring about the ideas of right and wrong? Who decides what is good or evil, if there is nothing outside of nature to establish it? Jean Paul Sartre said as much. Although himself an atheist, he said in *"existentialism is a humanism"*; "Existentialists on the other hand find it extremely disturbing that God no longer exists...there could no longer be any a priori good, since there would be no infinite and perfect consciousness to conceive of it."[52] (Sartre 2007)

EVALUATING A WORLDVIEW

Earlier, I let their own words describe for you the views presented by secular humanism. Douglas Groothius in Christian Apologetics wrote: "The credibility of a worldview is determined by whether or not arguments marshaled in its favor are compelling and logically consistent."[53] **(Groothius 2011)** In his book, he laid out the principle criteria agreed upon and utilized by philosophers to evaluate any worldview. Among those are internal logical consistency, existential viability, as well as intellectual and cultural fecundity. Based upon the core beliefs outlined in an

---

[52] Jean Paul Sartre, *Existentialism is a Humanism,* Carol Macomber trans., (New Haven: Yale University Press, 2007), 28

[53] Douglas Groothius, *Christian Apologetics,* (Downers Grove, IL: InterVarsity Press, 2011), 50

earlier chapter; let's objectively evaluate Secular Humanism.

Internal Logical Consistency-NOPE

First, secular humanism's epistemology is based on science as the best method for determining knowledge through observation, experimentation, and rational analysis as declared in the Humanist Manifesto III.

The scientific process begins with observation, leading to a hypothesis. Once a hypothesis is formed, it must be tested. Methods of experimentation must be developed to determine if that hypothesis is true or not. Only after multiple reproducible experiments, can something be considered a law. Yet, in the case of Darwinism, despite their being no reproducible experiments and no fossil records to support its claims; it has been declared a law which is readily accepted by secular humanists. While, at the same time, the Big

222

Bang Singularity theory proven by physicists through the expanding universe, the radiation echo and the second law of Thermodynamics was viewed with contempt and skepticism; because, it might give credence to the possibility of a creator God.[54] (Berlinski 2009). So, science is the end all for secular humanists; unless, true science fails to correspond to the secular humanist's other beliefs. *And they wonder why scientific relativism resulted from their promotion?*

Second, they also actively advocate for tolerance, social justice, and freedom of thought; unless, someone has a different view; particularly theism. Then they call the person bigoted, prejudiced and intolerant. Indeed, Paul Kurtz wrote about the common moral decencies including tolerance[55] on page 32 of *Multi-secularism;* after having spewed

---

[54] David Berlinski, *The Devil's Delusion,* (New York: Basic Books, 2009), 70-78.

[55] Kurtz, Multi-Secularism, 32

these words of hate toward Christianity on page 31. "The books of Abraham present the mythic figures of Moses (an imposing, patriarchal figure, offering the Promised Land to God's "chosen people"); Jesus (a bisexual, androgynous Son, sacrificed by God so that true believers can achieve "Rapture")"[56] (Kurtz 2010)

Third, they proclaim humans as moral beings; however, with Utilitarianism and Objective Morality from evolution, on what basis? Certainly, they condemn the atrocities of the Nazi's; although, the Society led by Hitler believed they were acting for the social good of the world, due to evolutionary superiority. Furthermore, they are against our prison systems holding so many, particularly the drug offenders; while, at the same time not considering the social implications of higher crime, rape, and murder because of the drug cartels.

---

[56] Kurtz, MultiSecularism,31

Fourth, despite proclaiming "We need to cultivate ethical wisdom and to appreciate the intrinsic value of life for its own sake."[57] (Kurtz 2010) Yet, the secular humanist at the same time is pro-abortion, pro-suicide, and pro-euthanasia. *How does that appreciate the intrinsic value of life?*

CONCLUDING THOUGHTS

With so many internal inconsistencies, how did the Secular Humanists gain such power in transforming our thoughts as a society? The answer is: we invited them in with an open door, even into our churches. Note all the changes within our own thought patterns, while attempting to win the crowds. All too often, to appear tolerant; we quickly lay aside our own fundamental truths. Instead of Christian counseling for marriages, we provide divorce care; accepting that

---

[57] Kurtz, Multi-Secularism, 32

divorce is a norm. So many now preach the prosperity, feel good gospel; presenting God as a Santa Claus, ignoring the reality that we live within a fallen world and that our Savior suffered.

Furthermore, we embraced the ideas that we must create an environment for our children in which they do not face reality, for fear it will hurt their ego. We foolishly accepted the false idea that we cannot point out the reality of sin in the hearts of men and women; for fear they might not "feel good" about themselves or we could irreparably bruise their ego with the truth. Forsaking the truth, we stopped believing and teaching that true joy, hope, and righteousness can ONLY be found when we come to END of ourselves and embrace God. Only in Him can we become the true royalty He created us to be. Often, that transformation comes through hardship and trials as we journey in the here and now through this broken world where evil does exist.

Beyond that, look at how many Christians flocked to "50 Shades of Grey". I have heard them say it is because they longed to see how the love of Anastasia transformed Christian Grey. True, God's love can transform a heart; but, a warped view of human love cannot. I am merely speaking from what I have heard; because, I did not want to read the book or see the movie. All too well, I knew the emotional scars of abuse which only God can heal. Only God's love can truly transform a heart, heal such wounds, and provide a means of true love.

So, desperately; we want to believe the lies of Satan. We want to believe that "without God" we are good, kind, truthful, and benevolent. Instead of seeking God's Grace, we want to stand as good ourselves; deserving everything beautiful and joyous.

Do we not realize, that our longing to be; comes from our own lack of being without God? Only in Him can we find our way. Only in Him can we discover the truest, purest love.

Meaning and Purpose Without God? Impossible!

As a worldview Secular Humanism lacks internal consistency as already demonstrated in the previous section. Furthermore, it lacks what is called philosophical existential viability. Existential has to do with existing. Philosophical existential viability deals with the innermost workings of human desires and how they enter act with the world around us. For existence to be viable within a society; existing must also provide meaning and purpose. Therein lies the questions. Why does mankind even exist? What could possibly be the purpose of life itself? Where do we find meaning and purpose?

The secular humanist believes that there is only the here and now and we must reach for our highest joy and fulfillment, now. However, for many, that thought is considered unlivable. Erich Fromm, a humanist himself was "sympathetic to religion. If every society, he thought, needs what he called a 'framework of orientation' or 'object of devotion' the consequences, when traditional objects of devotion are withdrawn or disappear, can be disastrous – leading to such aberrations in the twentieth century as Nazism and Stalinism. He described this condition in a figurative way as a form of 'necrophilia'"[58] (Benthall 2008)

Although, secular humanists believe that we can all reach a state of joy, self-actualization, and

---

[58] Jonathan Benthall, *Returning to Religion: Why a Secular Age is Haunted by Faith,* (London: I.B. Tauris, 2008), 10.

fulfillment in this life; they have yet to find a means to that end for more than only a few. Many of their own leaders found that to be the case. Maslow died, having never found his own self-actualization. Nietzsche lived his final years in an insane asylum. Jean Paul Sartre "denounced atheism on his deathbed as philosophically unlivable." [59] (Zacharias 2008)

Philosophical Existential Viability

For a worldview to have philosophical existential viability, it must be able to address reality and not just cling to some panacea of what might be. For the secular humanist, humans are thought to be innately good, and evil exists because of society not allowing that good to flourish. *However, who makes up society?* If society is made up of human beings; then, is it not logical that human beings are the source

---

[59] Ravi Zacharias, *The End of Reason*, (Grand Rapids, MI: Zondervan, 2008),43.

of evil itself? If my propensity to lie or feel anger is all due to my parents or society; then, I cannot be held culpable for any evil I perform. Even the existentialists recognized this truth. Unless we confront the evil within our own hearts; how can we change?

Jean Paul Sartre stated, "when an existentialist describes a coward, he says that the coward is responsible for his own cowardice. He is not the way he is because he has a cowardly heart, lung or brain. He is not like that as a result of his physiological makeup; he is like that because he has made himself a coward through his actions"[60] (Sartre 2007) The same is true of evil actions. Therefore, the one performing the evil or cowardice actions must be personally responsible for those actions. As Douglas Groothius points out, "If a worldview leads habitually to philosophical hypocrisy, it is rationally disqualified,

---

[60] Jean Paul Sartre, *Existentialism is a Humanism,* Carol Macomber trans., (New Haven: Yale University Press, 2007), 38

since this indicates that it does not correspond to reality."[61] (Groothius 2011)

Intellectual and Cultural Fecundity

Another criterion by which any worldview must be measured is its intellectual and cultural fecundity. In other words, does it lead to a better society? Do the beliefs held actually make a difference in the nation or world surrounding them for the good.

Secular humanism rose rapidly in the USA during the 1990s and won many battles in the Supreme court including removing prayer from the schools on June 25, 1962 (Engel v Vitale), legalizing abortion in 1973 (Roe vs Wade), and the sexual revolution beginning in the 1960s. Furthermore, despite proclaiming themselves as a nontheistic religion for purposes of taxes and winning that case in the Supreme

---

[61] Douglas Groothius, *Christian Apologetics,* (Downers Grove, IL: InterVarsity Press, 2011), 56

Court, (*Torcaso vs Watkins, 1961*); the secular humanist won in lower courts cases demanding that the Evolution theory be taught exclusively with the banning of the Creation theory as an alternative view. In other words, they gained the rights as a religion under the free exercise clause, to avoid taxes, and were deemed not a religion under the establishment clause.

The battle won in the supreme court regarding removing prayers from the schools; actually, only dealt with "organized prayer". It only said that a school could not have a "written prayer that all children must participate in" To a great extent, I would agree. However, instead of reading what the supreme court ruling actually said, Christians have cowered from the extreme leftist, fueled by the secular humanists into believing no prayers can be allowed. That is not at all what the supreme court ruling said. Despite that, we have allowed them to say that "no prayer can be on school campuses, voluntary or involuntary." Furthermore, they push to have the Bible banned on all campuses. That had nothing to do with the case they won in court.

WHAT HAPPENED NEXT?

After, the Bible and prayer were banned from the schools, we have watched the rise in violence in the schools, such as Columbine, the rise in rape, teenage suicide, alcohol abuse, and drug abuse among our teens. Our college campuses have seen violent protests against any conservative speaker or conservative teachers (the few that can be found).

The legalization of abortions has led to millions of potential lives being killed before they can even begin. Furthermore, as we saw in the Presidential debates of 2016; there is an ever-increasing push for partial birth abortions in which a sharp instrument is stabbed into the baby's head to kill it before delivery or hypertonic saline is injected into the womb causing a slow and painful death of the fetus over a period of days.

Furthermore, the sexual revolution has led to increasing numbers of single parent homes, resulting in expanding numbers of children growing up in poverty, despair, and hopelessness. HIV which began in Africa, having been contracted from the chimpanzee; spread rapidly due to prostitution throughout the trade routes in Congo and later spread throughout the world easily with our sexually enlightened society.

MEANING AND PURPOSE

As shown, secular humanism has failed to provide meaning and purpose for our existence as individuals. It has certainly failed with each step of its experimentation toward a better society. Yet, meaning and purpose can be found in the gospel message. The

Bible provides us with the hope we so desperately need. Only there do we discover our true meaning and purpose to live.

And we have such trust through Christ toward God. Not that we are sufficient of ourselves to think of anything as being from ourselves, but our sufficiency is from God, (2 Corinthians 3:4-5, NKJV)

2 Corinthians 3:6-12 (TLB)

> *He is the one who has helped us tell others about his new agreement to save them. We do not tell them that they must obey every law of God or die; but, we tell them there is life for them from the Holy Spirit. The old way, trying to be saved by keeping the Ten Commandments, ends in death; in the new way, the Holy Spirit gives them life.*

Yet that old system of law that led to death began with such glory that people could not bear to look at Moses' face. For as he gave them God's law to obey, his face shone out with the very glory of God-though the brightness was already fading away. Shall we not expect far greater glory in these days when the Holy Spirit is giving life? If the plan that leads to doom was glorious, much more glorious is the plan that makes men right with God.

In fact, that first glory as it shone from Moses' face is worth nothing at all in comparison with the overwhelming glory of the new agreement. So, if the old system that faded into nothing was full of heavenly glory, the glory of God's new plan for our salvation is certainly far greater, for it is eternal. Since we know that this new glory will never go away, we can preach with great boldness.

BECAUSE OF JESUS CHRIST

Now the Lord is the Spirit; and where the Spirit of the Lord is, there is liberty. But we all, with unveiled face, beholding as in a mirror the glory of the Lord, are being transformed into the same image from glory to glory, just as by the Spirit of the Lord (2 Corinthians 3:17-18).

Chapter 23

Christianity as a Worldview

How does Christianity stand as a Worldview when placed under the microscope of Internal Consistency, Existential Viability, as well as, Intellectual and Cultural Fecundity? Since these were the criteria under which we examined the Secular Humanists, I believe it only fair to evaluate Christianity by these same three.

Internal Consistency

Christianity presents a never changing, omnipotent God as creator and sustainer of the Universe. The story presented throughout the scripture is unchanging and consistent from Genesis to Revelation; despite it being written over thousands of years by many writers. The story has not changed. God has remained constant. God created mankind with free will, man chooses evil, God's grace redeems those who choose His gift of grace. He consistently continues to reveal Himself.

In the Old Testament, He revealed Himself through nature, special revelations and the prophets in the Old Testament. God revealed things before they happened through His prophets with perfect accuracy. He forewarned the people; before judgment would befall them, and always provided them a means to escape the impending trials. If only, they would turn from their sin and seek Him; He would provide a way of salvation. Even when they utterly failed; God remained faithful to His covenant and would draw them back to Himself.

Knowing that the only hope of true fulfillment, joy, and love were found in a relationship with Him; God did and continues to do everything to bring that about. Daniel even told of the very day Jesus would ride into Jerusalem in Daniel 9:25-26, long before the event would occur. How did He know? God revealed it to Him. God continues to reveal Himself today through nature, through scientific discoveries, archeological finds, and through our ability to experience goodness, joy, and love.

The critics would say that there are many inconsistencies within the Bible; however, a careful study of the scripture shows that just not to be true. Furthermore, critics want to say the manuscripts must have been altered over time; however, "manuscripts that are part of the Dead Sea Scrolls, for instance, clearly show that our modern copies of the Old Testament are incredibly accurate."[62] (Velarde)

Furthermore, there is nothing more profound concerning the internal consistency of Christianity, than the life, the teaching, the death, and the

---

[62] Robert Velarde, "Is the Bible Reliable", Focusonthefamily.com, accessed 1/8/2018. https://www.focusonthefamily.com/faith/the-study-of-god/how-do-we-know-the-bible-is-true/is-the-bible-reliable

resurrection of Jesus Christ. Those who discover the gospel of Jesus Christ, "find a truth that is both humbling and ennobling. The saving truth of Jesus Christ is a gift of God's grace. As sinners we can only receive it in humility. Yet Jesus declared that the gospel is a truth that sets us free (John 8:31-32). [63] (Groothius 2011).

Existential Viability

Christianity provides a message of hope, joy, and peace; even amid tragedies. Because Christians live within a relationship with God who speaks with them, guides them, provides for them, and comforts them; they can face great trials with hope and joy in their heart. The gospel message makes life livable, here and now. As Douglas Groothius wrote: "A true worldview should be livable; it should not commit us to

---

[63] Groothius, *Apologetics*, 146

perpetual intellectual and moral frustration"[64] (Groothius 2011) No other worldview provides such a message of hope and livability as does Christianity. Furthermore, within each individual human on this planet, we find a desire for something much greater than our own existence. That is the true search for being; rather, than a mere existence on this planet. Just as Paul so aptly spoke of in Acts 17:24-28

> *God that made the world and all things therein, seeing that He is Lord of heaven and earth, dwelleth not in temples made with hands; neither is worshipped with men's hands, as though he needed any thing seeing he giveth to all life, and breath, and all things; And hath made of one blood all nations of men for to dwell on all the face of the earth, and that*

---

[64] Groothius, *Apologetics,* 136

determined the times before appointed, and the bounds of their habitation; that they should seek the Lord, if haply they might feel after him, and find him, though he be not far from every one of us: For in Him we live, and move, and have our being

The fact that we are born with desires for more than mere existence, desires that transcend our mere hope to survive, suggests that there is something much greater than our mundane existence. To make that existence livable; we too must transcend beyond our day by day existence. This is what C.S. Lewis referred to when he wrote:

"Creatures are not born with desires unless satisfaction for those desires exists. If I find in myself a desire which no experience in this world can satisfy, the most probable explanation is that I was made for another world. If none of my early pleasures satisfy it, that does not prove that the universe is a fraud. Probably earthly desires were never meant to satisfy it, but only to arouse it, to suggest the real thing"[65] (Lewis 1952)

Even Jean Paul Sartre wrote, although himself an atheist, we "find it extremely disturbing that God no longer exits, for along with his disappearance goes the possibility of finding values in an intelligible heaven."[66] (Sartre 2007) Jonathan Benthall, himself a secularist, suggests there is a void that occurs which must be filled when we remove religion from the world. He goes on to say, "Reason tells us that what separates human

---

[65] C.S. Lewis, *Mere Christianity,* 1944 reprint, (New York: Simon & Schuster, 1996), 121
[66] Sartre, *Existentialism,* 28

beings from animals is precisely – short of some future extraordinary discoveries by neurobiologists – the elusive stuff, whether it is poetry or electronic bank transfers."[67] (Benthall 2008)

Furthermore, we find on the back-cover description of Returning *to Religion: Why a Secular Age is Haunted by Faith* these words: "A human universal, the religious inclination underlies the fabric of who and what we are: we cannot choose to repudiate it, only how to channel it."[68] (Benthall 2008) He suggests there is a need for religious substitutes or 'religiod' (religious like) activities. But, if there is truly within humans a religious inclination; doesn't that indicate there is much more to mankind that the mere evolutionary changes of atoms? Why must we search for substitutes, rather than recognize that God placed that desire in our hearts that we might find Him?

---

[67] Benthall, Haunted by Faith, 18
[68] Ibid., back cover

Intellectual and Cultural Growth Really is a Christian Thing

Having evaluated Christianity for its internal consistency and existential viability, let us turn to evaluate its intellectual and cultural fecundity. In other words, does it produce an abundance of growth and help humanity to flourish both intellectually and culturally. Indeed, it has been the Christian faith that led the way in scientific discovery; because, Christians believe that God is a God who reveals Himself to humanity through nature, rigorous study, and through personal enlightenment. Princeton, Yale and Harvard were originally founded as Christian Universities; although, their founders would be appalled by how much they have changed. "While some have pitted faith against reason, the Bible does not endorse blind leaps of faith in the dark but rather speaks of the *knowledge of God* gained through various rational

247

means. Instead of a *leap* of faith, it commends a well-informed and volitional *step* of faith"[69] (Groothius 2011)

A careful review of history reveals that the Christians led the way in scientific and industrial exploration. Although, there may have been a time period in which the Catholic Church tried to restrict the knowledge as a means of "power control"; it was Christians such as Galileo "who discerned no discord between the Bible and natural science."[70] (Groothius 2011) Instead of Christians hiding under a cloak of ignorance, we are taught to study and defend the faith intellectually. Christ, himself; through the knowledge of Old Testament Scripture stood firm against Satan when tempted. Additionally, His discourse with the Pharisees and Sadducees of His day were carried out intellectually. He set the example for all of us to follow.

---

[69] Groothius, Apologetics, 96
[70] Ibid, 100

Flourishing Cultural Growth

True Christians have stood as the beacon of light for charity throughout the world. The Bible teaches that we are to care for the poor, the widows, and the sick. Indeed, the Humanist Manifesto I states, "this age does owe a vast debt to the traditional religions". Why? Because True Christians laid out the foundations and principles on which society should stand. However, despite the secular humanists recognizing this; they then try to denounce faith as though it were evil. Christopher Hitchens wrote as one of his four objections to Christianity as being, "that it is both the cause and the result of dangerous sexual repression." [71] (Hitchens 2009) So, repressing one's sexual desires is dangerous to whom? Society or the individual? Learning to repress one's sexual desires, except in

---

[71] Christopher Hitchens, *God is Not Great,* (New York: Hachette Book Group, 2009), 4

marriage, as designed; would eliminate rape, sexual abuse, and truly enhance the union of the marriage as the pleasures are greater when experienced by two people who have the ecstasy of uniting as one in love, having this experience held uniquely with each other.

The secularists, also, try to point to atrocities during the middle ages and tragedies proclaimed in the name of Christ as a reason not to believe. However, when they do so, they are pointing out terrors performed by sinful men; who proclaimed the name of Christ, not the message of Christianity itself. However, Christ Himself, spoke of these men in Matthew 7:22-24. Terrible things over the ages of time have been done in the "name of Christianity"; however, that is not True Christianity. Unfortunately, broken, sin filled men and women, professing to be Christians often provide the greatest reasons for others to not believe. Yet, if we look at our own country's rich history, we would discover that it was Christians who fought to free the people from England, fought to free the slaves, fought for women's rights, and provide many relief efforts around the world.

The secularists, also try to say that secular humanism has led to a greater good. However, have they forgotten the history of the twentieth century? As David Berlinski wrote: "Just who has imposed on the suffering human race poison gas, barbed wire, high explosives, experiments in eugenics, the formula for Zyklon B, heavy artillery, pseudo-scientific justifications for mass murder, cluster bombs, attack submarines, napalm, intercontinental ballistic missiles, military space platforms, and nuclear weapons? If memory serves, it was not the Vatican."[72] (Berlinski 2009)

---

[72] David Berlinski, *The Devil's Delusion,* (New York: Basic Books, 2009), 21

RACISM

The secularists love to use words such as racism or bigotry to denounce Christians; because, they know those words are like a knife stabbing into our hearts. The reason those words cause us such pain, is they do not reflect the truth of the gospel message in any way, shape or form. They cause the Christians to retreat, reflect on all they have said, and wonder how their words or deeds could have been so misconstrued. The Bible teaches so strongly against racism and bigotry. It teaches us to love all mankind as being created by God. We are to preach the gospel to all nations (Matthew 28:19-20). Or as Paul pointed out God *"hath made of one blood all nations"* (Acts 17:26).

Yet, it is the secular humanists who teach the evolutionary principles of "survival of the fittest." It was this evolutionary ideology that caused Hitler to decide it was a good idea to annihilate an entire group of people. Indeed, the very idea of evolution (a theory never proven in the laboratories of science or archeology); which, believes that some human beings have evolved to be superior over others. Their own push toward aborting fetuses that are not perfect or euthanasia of those who do not give back to society; shows that these ideologies of racism and bigotry are theirs, not the Christians.

Furthermore, they support the idea of allowing illegal immigration; so that we might have a new form of slavery in order to supply our ever-growing need of food, cheaply or to gain political power through keeping the oppressed, oppressed in need of their "charity." You only have to have lived among the illegal immigrants and the Mexican people to come to realize how they are really treated and the lifestyle they are forced to live in; due to poverty. Oh, yes; they are given fake documents and social security numbers, do vote, get free healthcare; but, are left as the disposables by those who want them here to provide cheap labor and political power through voting.

I lived in Mexico for several years, my visa did NOT allow me to work-I was only provided permission to live there as a wife and mother. I could not work, and my Visa was set to expire, when my husband passed away. There was no chance for amnesty, if I had wanted to stay. I was there when President Bill Clinton caused Mexico's emerging middle class to be destroyed because of his trade deals with China. Along with the Mexican people, I lost everything I financially owned that December 1994. Only through keeping the poor people poor in Mexico; could the people be manipulated and used by the far left.

We can do far more to help the Mexican people, if we are strong financially as a nation; instead, of exploiting their poor for our gain.

INTELLECTUAL AND CULTURAL GROWTH:
A CHRISTIAN THING

Why, given the truth of history and the gospel message, have we Christians cowed to the criticisms launched as us by the secularists? Ah, that is easy. We recognize that we are flawed; because, we understand that it is God's grace which saved us. Looking deep within our own hearts we see the blemishes there; but, God never meant for us to become silenced by our own weaknesses. Instead, that is part of the good news which should make us bold in proclaiming the gospel to the world. We are all broken and in need of a Savior. For that reason, we must study, grow, pray and rest upon the power of the Holy Spirit to guide us.

Go forth boldly then to be the light and salt of the world, knowing that we hold the key to wisdom in Jesus Christ. We can make a difference in the world;

by spreading the goodness of God. Yet, we do it with humility; knowing that without Him, we can do nothing. (I Corinthians 4:4, 8:2, 9:16). However, we can do all things through Christ who strengthens us. (Philippians 4:13).

Chapter 24

How to Defend Your Faith

Never in the course of American history have Christians been under such direct attack for their faith than now. As pointed out earlier, to a great extent our silence on these matters has led to our reaching this point in history. So, we cannot continue in silence and hope for the best. We must learn how to respond and to defend our faith; if we are to remain the salt and light to a world in desperate need of the gospel message, before our voices are silenced forever. That requires study on our part.

We must prayerfully study God's Word that we might be ready when questioned to respond with intellectually sound defense arguments. Furthermore, we must teach our children to do the same. There is no question anymore whether our faith will be attacked;

257

instead, the question is when and if we will be prepared to answer. For that reason, I want to help you gain the hunger to know more and give you some examples of what I mean by being prepared to defend your faith.

Of all the questions levied against the Christian faith, the problem of evil is perhaps the one most used. Because of that, I want to confront that one first.

THE PROBLEM OF EVIL

Basically put, the problem of evil presents itself in the question: "why would an Almighty, all knowing good God allow such evil to exist in the world?" Evil does exist; as we are all aware. Evil and suffering exists all around us. It presents itself in natural disasters such as hurricanes, earthquakes, tornados, flooding and drought for example. Furthermore, we see evil presented at the hands of human beings too numerous to count: mass murders, terrorist attacks, rape, lies, selfishness, and theft, to name a few. As Groothius points out, "Human cruelty is all around us; we will find it within ourselves as well."[73] (Groothius 2011). Then, there is the problem with disease and all its suffering. Even, the staunchest Christian is not exempt from suffering and the effects of evil. How then can we Christians say, "God is good, loving and all powerful;" if so much evil exists?

That perhaps is the question we are asked most often by the secularists. And it is the question our own hearts may ask at times; unless, we have come to recognize the truth so richly presented in the scripture. So, the argument presented by the secularists goes like this as presented by Groothius from his outline of Epicurus.

---

[73] Groothius, *Apologetics,* 615

God either wishes to take away evil, and is unable; or he is able and unwilling; or he is neither willing or able, or he is both willing and able.[74] (Groothius 2011).

Epicurus then tries to work out each possibility

1. If God is willing and is unable, he is feeble, which is not in accordance with the character of God.

2. If he is able and unwilling, he is envious (meaning evil), which is equally at variance with God.

3. If he is neither willing nor able he is both envious (meaning evil) and feeble, and therefore not God.

4. If he is both willing and able, which alone is suitable to God, from what source then are evils or why does he not remove them?[75]

---

[74] Groothius, *Apologetics,* 616
[75] Ibid.

The secularists take this one step further to say; therefore, there is no God.

RESPONDING TO THE PROBLEM OF EVIL

As a Christian, I have faced many trials due to evil, including abuse, cancer, chronic illness, multiple surgeries, financial disasters, as well as witnessing the suffering of my mother and husband due to bipolar disease. So, this is a question I have confronted throughout my life; yet, I can loudly confirm that God is fully able (all powerful) and is fully loving in having allowed evil to exist. He is wiser than we could ever imagine; and, as a loving God, He desires His creation to discover the greatest joy and happiness. Therefore, He endures the personal suffering of evil Himself, in order to allow us to discover that greater joy in Him. There are four major arguments to come to that conclusion which I wish to present for you.

Let me begin by pointing out that we cannot truly see or know what good is; if we have never experienced what the absence of good (evil) is. Just as darkness is the absence of light; evil is the absence of good. God did not create evil; however, because God is perfect goodness and righteousness-there stands to reason evil presents as a void of God's righteousness.

THE ARGUMENT FOR FREE WILL

When God created the world and placed man in the garden of Eden; everything was perfect. God walked with Adam every day; yet, for Adam to truly experience that pleasure and to be able to love God truly, he was provided free will to choose. For that reason, God placed the tree of the knowledge of good and evil in the garden. Adam was told not to eat thereof. Therefore, a choice was provided to either trust God's word or to choose to disobey God. Obviously, if Adam fully cherished the wonder and beauty of what he possessed in that relationship with God, he could not have disobeyed; however, he did not fully cherish his relationship with God, until it was gone. Only then could he truly experience God's love, righteousness, and glory; but, to do so also meant he could see the evil present in God's absence.

C. S. Lewis wrote in mere Christianity:

> God created things which had free will. That means creatures can go either wrong or right. Some people think they can imagine a creature which was free but had no possibility of going wrong; I cannot. If a thing is free to be good it is also free to be bad. And free will is what has made evil possible. Why, then, did God give them free will? Because free will though it makes evil possible, is also the only thing that makes possible any love

or goodness or joy worth having. A world of automata-of creatures that worked like machines-would hardly be worth creating.

The happiness which God designs for His higher creatures is the happiness of being freely, voluntarily united to Him and to each in an ecstasy of love delight compared with which the most rapturous love between a man and a woman on this earth is mere milk and water. And for that they must be free.[76] (C. Lewis 1952)

Without free will, we could never understand nor experience perfect love, joy, hope, or glory. Instead we would be like robots wandering about the planet

---

[76] C.S. Lewis, *Mere Christianity,* (New York: HarperCollins, 1952), 47-48

with no depth of feeling and no reasoning. Lewis goes on to say:

> Of course, God knew what would happen if they used their freedom the wrong way: apparently, He thought it worth the risk. Perhaps we feel inclined to disagree with Him. But there is a difficulty about disagreeing with God. He is the source from which all your reasoning power comes: you could not be right, and He wrong any more than a stream can rise higher than its own source. When you are arguing against Him you are arguing against the very power that makes you able to argue at all: it is like cutting off the branch you are sitting on. If God thinks this state of war in the universe a price worth paying for

free will—that is, for making a live world in which creatures can do real good or harm and something of real importance can happen, instead of a toy world which only moves when He pulls the strings— then we may take it is worth paying.[77] (C. Lewis 1952)

Therefore, God was never the author of evil; yet, when given the freedom to choose, Adam chose sin through his own volition. Every human being since then is presented with the same choice. That we are free to choose; then, no longer can we blame God, rather it is our own choice. Indeed, God could have brought immediate judgment upon the earth; after all, He could see through the corridors of time all the evil that men and women would choose. However, He also could see through the corridors of time, everyone who

---

[77] Lewis, *Christianity,* 47-48

would accept His gift of salvation. His overwhelming love for each and every one of them caused Him to stay His hand of judgment. He continues to steady His hand, today. Had He not, you nor I would be here to even discuss this.

He could have just turned His back upon the whole of creation. However, He did not do that either. Instead, He provided a way for man to choose Him through faith. From Genesis until now; God has provided a way for mankind to be saved from the evil within their own hearts and the world around them, through faith in Jesus Christ. The Old Testament looked forward to His coming by faith; and we, look back to see His completed work. As Paul presented in Romans, everyone is given a chose; because, God reveals Himself to each. Read Paul's defense:

For I am not ashamed of the gospel of Christ: for it is the power of

God unto salvation to every one that believeth; .... For therein is the righteousness of God revealed from faith to faith: as it is written, the just shall live by faith. For the wrath of God is revealed from heaven against all ungodliness and unrighteousness of men, who hold the truth in unrighteousness; Because that which may be known of God is manifest in them; for God hath shewed it unto them. For the invisible things of him from the creation of the world are clearly seen, being understood by the things that are made, even his eternal power and Godhead; so that they are without excuse: Because that, when they knew God, they glorified him not as God, neither were thankful; but became vain in their imaginations, and their foolish heart was darkened. Professing themselves to be wise, they became fools, who changed the truth of God into a lie, and worshipped and served the creature more than the Creator. (Romans 1:16-25).

SECOND DEFENSE TO THE PROBLEM OF EVIL

The second defense is that of "the Greater Good" defense. As I presented at the beginning of this chapter and throughout the previous defense, evil serves a purpose; whether, we fully comprehend it or not. Augustine addressed it in this manner,

For the Almighty God, who, as even the heathen acknowledge, has supreme power over all things, being Himself supremely good, would never permit the existence of anything evil among His works, if He were not so omnipotent and good that He can bring good even out of evil"[78] (Augustine 1961)

That has been precisely the case in my own life. Of a certainty, I would not fully know the joy, hope, and love which I experience now; had it not been for the trials I have faced in this journey. Every step of the way, God has drawn me nearer to Him. There, I have found the sweetness of knowing His grace. Through it all, He has provided me with glimpses of His Glory; while, at the same time transforming my own heart. He has sifted away the chaff, revealed the darkness or evil of my own selfishness and has been steadily at work transforming me into the likeness of Christ. Though He has a lot more work to do; I realize how precious it

---

[78] Augustine, *Enchiridion on Faith, Hope, and Love*, trans. J.F. Shaw, (Chicago: Henry Reguery, 1961), 11

is that one day I will stand before Him with a heart like that of my Savior.

Yet, no one more profoundly presents this truth than Joni Eareckson Tada. I would encourage you to go to YouTube and listen to any of her tapes. Particularly, I recommend her True Woman '14 Conference. In it she refers to suffering as God's lemon juice being squeezed over our hearts; transforming us. Also, she says; "there is no trial too great to face in order to know Jesus."

Or as Paul wrote:

For I reckon that the sufferings of this present time are not worthy to be compared with the glory which shall be revealed in us. (Romans 8:18)

Yea doubtless, and I count all things but loss for the excellency of the knowledge of Christ Jesus my Lord: for whom I have suffered the loss of all things, and do count them but dung, that I may win Christ (Philippians 3:8).

God has a purpose and a plan which is for our good. Evil exists in this world; yet, without it would I really know the ecstasy of knowing Jesus. Only God can take a broken life, filled with wrong choices and still make it one filled with hope, love and joy.

THIRD DEFENSE FOR THE PROBLEM OF EVIL

The third defense is cumulative, standing upon the previous two. It was presented by Jonathan Edwards and explains how it was necessary for our ultimate joy that God allow evil to exist in the world. I will let it stand upon its own merits; because, of all the defenses, this one was the one that shone into my heart during many years of suffering; providing me with the understanding I needed to rejoice, even in my suffering. Jonathan Edwards wrote this with such clarity, that any attempt to explain it would demonstrate my own ineptness to express it as well. Here is what he wrote:

> It is a proper and excellent thing for infinite glory to shine forth; and for the same reason, it is proper that the shining forth of God's glory be complete; that is, that all parts of his glory should shine forth, that every beauty should be proportionably effulgent (=radiant), that the beholder may have a proper notion of God. It is not proper that one glory should be exceedingly manifested, and another not at all....
>
> Thus, it is necessary, that God's awful majesty, his authority and dreadful greatness, justice, and holiness, should

be manifested. But this could not be, unless sin and punishment had been decreed; so that the shining forth of God's glory would be very imperfect, both because these parts of divine glory would not shine forth as the others do, and also the glory of his goodness, love, and holiness would be faith without them; nay, they could scarcely shine forth at all.

If it were not right that God should decree and permit and punish sin, there could be no manifestation of God's holiness in hatred of sin, or in showing any preference, in his providence, of godliness before it. There would be no manifestation of God's grace or true goodness, if there was no sin to be pardoned, no misery to be saved from.

How much happiness so ever he bestowed, his goodness would not be so much prized and admired, and the sense of it not so great....

So, evil is necessary, in order to the highest happiness of the creature and the completeness of that communication of God, for which he made the world; because the creature's happiness consists in the knowledge of God, and the sense of his love. And if the knowledge of him be imperfect, the happiness of the creature must be proportionably imperfect.[79] (Edwards 1974)

Reread this argument, pray fully; then, think about when you are confronted with the problem of

---

[79] Jonathan Edwards, "Concerning the Divine Decrees", *The Works of Jonathan Edwards,* (Edinburgh: Banner of Truth, 1974), 528

evil. I have found this argument as comforting to my soul. It is brought even into clearer focus when I consider what Paul wrote.

> *What if God, willing to shew his wrath, and to make his power known, endured with much longsuffering the vessels of wrath fitted to destruction: and that he might make known the riches of his glory on the vessels of mercy, which he had afore prepared unto glory* (Romans 9:22-23).

FOURTH DEFENSE

Essentially, the fourth defense is who determines what is evil and what is good, if there is no Superior Being, outside of man to determine what is good or evil? Can there be such a thing as good or evil if there is no God? Who determines that? Often, the secularist will say that it is determined by society. But, then which society? The militant Isis society would tell you that they are right. Hitler believed that he was right and the majority of the German people in that moment believed that to be true. If God does not exist; then, is everything permitted? If there is no foundation for that which is good; who determines what is good? Certainly, we see that in our modern world.

The far leftist movement shout loudly that they are "right" and everyone else is wrong; pronouncing judgment on everyone else. Much like Hollywood who seem suddenly outraged by the #METOO movement screaming against sexual predators while promoting the movie "Fifty Shades Freed", the third in a series of blatant sexual and emotional abuse of a young woman by a wealthy man. So, which is it?

Christians were lumped into a basket of deplorables; because, they cared about such things as life, denouncing abortion, constitutionalist supreme court judges, patriotism, laws, justice and middle America.

So, without God; where is the foundation for good and if there is none; then, who says what is evil or good? If the twentieth century taught us anything; then, we must recognize the atrocities of the atheistic regimes of Stalin, Hitler, and North Korea. Also, we must recognize the rise in drug abuse, suicide, and violent crime within our own nation. Neither the shooter in Las Vegas, nor the man who shot at the Republican Congressmen professed to be Christians.

Conclusion:

As I have presented, we are to be ready with a defense when we are attacked. That does require knowledge and an intense desire to study God's word, prayer fully allowing Him to reveal Himself to us. Silence is not an option.

CHAPTER 25

In Defense of God

Although, the problem of evil is perhaps one of the hardest to confront or respond to quickly. There are many other defenses for God's existence, many more than I could hope to cover in this one book. Although I do want to present for you a few more, just to whet your appetite to further study yourself.

Ontological Argument

The basis of this argument was formed initially by St. Anselm. It is a deductive reasoning which begins with the idea that within our subconscious, we conceive of a being that is greater than anything else. Indeed, our fascination with superheroes and our own drive to push toward grandeur, is such an idea. The fact that such a being is even conceptually supplanted in our minds, can lead us to believe that either he exists only in our mind or also in reality. It is greater to exist in reality; therefore, God exists not merely in the understanding, but also in reality.[80] (Groothius 2011)

The argument presented against this is that just because someone can conceive something; doesn't mean it exists. Perhaps; but, even atheists such as Carl Sagan or Paul Kurtz speak of viewing the sky, or a beautiful sunset with a feeling of awe and wonder. Why would human beings even experience awe or wonder? It is that kind of awe and wonder that Paul Kurtz refers to when he wrote that we are "part of a vast cosmic scene, a magnificent awe-inspiring universe that we can unravel and comprehend"[81] (Kurtz 2010) But, why do we even know wonder and awe? There has been no evidence to suggest that any of the animals upon this

---

[80] Groothius, *Apologetics*, 187-189
[81] Kurtz, Multi-secularism, 256

earth other than humans can conceive of grandeur, long for it, or desire to be in its presence.

Our consciousness of and desire for grandeur should cause one to wonder where that desire came from. It certainly did not come from a random mixing of atomic particles. Our ability to reason; suggests that we were created for a much higher purpose and our longing for glory suggests something far more glorious. How can I long for perfect righteousness, if there is no such thing? Or transcendent love?

The Cosmological Argument

For a long time, the belief was held that the Universe was constant. Many scientists, philosophers believed that the universe itself was eternal; although, even then there was a "faith" that something had existed eternally. Even if that something was some subatomic particle that somehow became the creator of all we now can see. Their faith was that sooner or later, science could find the answer of how everything arrived on earth as it is. But, it still begs the question, "Why is there something rather than nothing?"[82] (Groothius 2011)

However, with further exploration and discovery; all their theories were blown out of the water with the big bang singularity theory. Despite many scientists, physicists, and philosophers trying to dismiss the idea that the universe came into being suddenly; all of the scientific evidence began to pile up, until now, it is certain that the universe came into existence suddenly. The Big Bang Cosmology "was first predicted in esoteric equations and later confirmed through multiple layers of evidence. So, while the big ban cosmology is hardly Holy Writ, it is the prevailing incumbent, whose impeachment seems unlikely."[83]

---

[82] Groothius, *Apologetics*, 213
[83] Ibid., 230

(Groothius 2011) This despite desperate atheistic scientists trying with all their might to prove it wasn't so. However, the big bang appeared first in literature in Genesis 1.

Intelligent Design

Intelligent design "argues that key features of the regularly functioning natural world are best explained by the influence of design at some stage in the distant past."[84] (Groothius 2011) This is not a theory presented by theists only; however, many atheistic scientists have come to realize that there are complexities that cannot be explained. Indeed, Darwin had said that if such a complex organism could be found unexplainable by gradual mutations, his theory would break down.[85] (Groothius 2011). Naturally, the atheist are in search for other possibilities such as

---

[84] Groothius, *Apologetics*, 300
[85] Ibid., 308

aliens or other undiscovered universes; yet, the fact of intelligent design would have been necessary for the DNA molecule or the flagellum to exist. This leads to a strong case that the designer had to have surpassing intelligence. Even, the fact that we have the state of consciousness and intelligence to wonder about such things; begs, for an Almighty, Omniscient Creator.

Within the Ontological Arguments, the Cosmological Arguments, and the Intelligent Design Arguments; it is evident that there must have been a something outside of space (omnipresent), outside of time (eternal), and outside of energy/matter (omnipotent) to have caused the beginning the universe. That something had to be intelligent and had to be the greatest someone or something we could ever imagine, which by definition is God.

Defense of Objective Truth and Moral Values

What are the foundations for morality to begin with? Often, the secular humanist will try to say that because evil exists in the world, God cannot exist, or He is impotent, or He is unloving. That, however, is a different debate as presented in the previous chapter; yet, it does present the acknowledgement that evil and good do exist in the world. But then where is there a foundation for that? Can we say in a world formed through evolutionary means, that such an idea could exist at all? After all, do we consider it evil within the animal kingdom for one animal to murder, or to eat their own offspring to survive? Why would humans be any different, if survival, flourishing and pleasure are the ultimate goal? William Lane Craig in his debate with Paul Kurtz very clearly presented the case that "if theism is true, we have a sound foundation for morality"[86] (Craig 2009). He went to present three major points regarding this in his opening statement. 1) To say, "that there are objective moral values is to say that something is good or evil independently of whether anybody believes it to be so."[87] 2) "if theism is true, we have a sound basis for objective moral duties"[88] 3) "if, theism is true, we have a sound basis for moral accountability"[89]

Often the arguments presented by the secular humanist is that "you don't have to believe in God to be good." Certainly, we know that is true. Furthermore, we have all seen many professing Christians, who commit horrendous acts. But that is not the question. The question is why is there any moral code or

---

[86] William Lane Craig, "The Kurtz/Craig Debate: Is Goodness without God Good Enough?" *Is Goodness Without God Good Enough?: A Debate on Faith, Secularism, and Ethics,* (Lanham, MD: Rowman & Littlefield Publishers, 2009), 30.

[87] Ibid.

[88] Ibid.

[89] Ibid., 31

goodness, were there not a God. As Groothius wrote, "we need to find a worldview that accounts for the origin, existence and knowledge of such good and such evil, and provides us sufficient moral motivation to pursue good and oppose evil. The basic argument from goodness to deity is fairly simple.

1. If a personal God does not exist, then objective moral values do not exist.

2. Objective moral values do exist.

3. Therefore, a personal God exists"[90] (Groothius 2011)

The areas of defense I have thus far presented are for the existence of God and some basics of the Christian Faith. However, no defense of Christianity is more important than being able to defend the

---

[90] Groothius, *Apologetics,* 345

resurrection of Jesus Christ. Therefore, I would want to include that also as follows.

HE IS RISEN INDEED

Without the resurrection of Jesus Christ, Christianity would be a hopeless faith, leaving mankind forever lost in his sin. It is for that reason, every Christian needs to be prepared to defend the death, burial and resurrection of Jesus Christ to a world of skeptics with facts and not just because "the Bible tells me so." For that reason, this discussion, will present the case for Christ Jesus, as the risen Lord; based on the evidence, drawing the best logical conclusion of the data as compared to the various theories presented by the skeptics. Although, scriptures will be used; for this discussion, they will be treated as historical accounts by eye witnesses, rather than as God inspired.

Death on the Cross

Before any discussion of resurrection, one must begin with death; because, for there to be a resurrection, one must have died. "It is a well-established fact that Jesus died by crucifixion in the early 30s."[91] (Groothius 2011) His death is written about, not only in Matthew, Mark, Luke and John; but, is also reported by the letters of Paul, the sermons recorded in Acts, and the writing of James. Furthermore, it is recorded by Josephus, a Jewish Priest who went on to become a historian; having joined the Romans (even in battle against the Jews) and adopting the last name of Flavius, the family name of the Roman Emperor. He wrote about the death of Jesus in his Antiquities of the Jews 18.3.3. Tactius, another secular historian who held Christians in contempt; also, reported the death of Jesus in his

---

[91] Groothius, *Apologetics,* 540.

Annals as fact. Despite this, some would propose the "swoon theory" that Jesus had not died or as Islam, that Allah miraculously substituted another person on the cross and made them appear to be Jesus.

Neither of these theories hold any credibility. Death on the cross, was very cruel and the Centurions carrying out this sentence were experts in death. Crucifixion death occurs by asphyxiation, when the person is unable to pull or push their body up to take a breath. Unlike the thieves beside him, Jesus had been severely flogged and beaten with whips containing steel bits that tore his flesh from his ribcage, had not been given any food or water; and therefore, "was so weakened by his beetings that he was unable to carry his cross all the way to Golgotha, the execution site (Matthew 27:32)"[92] (Groothius 2011). His severe state of hypovolemia from blood loss with the addition of

---

[92] Groothius, *Apologetics,* 541.

excrutiating pain, left him in a near shock state, too weak to pull or push his body upward. Beyond that, when the Centurion thrust the spear in his side; both, water and blood poured forth (John 19:34, I John 5:6,8). The only possibilty for water and blood would be a pericardial and/or pulmonary effusion; with the spear piercing either the aorta or the heart itself. This medical fact, John would not have even known. Yet, as a true witness of the event, he recorded what he saw. John was the only apostle standing at the foot of the cross. No human body could have survived the final piercing of the sword; even if, not already dead as confirmed by the Centurion (John 19:33, Mark 15:45).

Furthermore, the "miraculous substitution" idealogy was an ad hoc to be able to maintain Jesus as a prophet, not the son of God; confirming that someone certainly died on that cross that day who was proclaimed to be Jesus Christ. Remember too, that the women had followed every step of the way from his arrest, beatings, to the cross, and even to his burial.

The Burial

"Besides his death, scholars agree that Jesus was buried in a tomb owned by Joseph of Arimathea"[93] (Groothius 2011). Most criminals who were crucified in that day were placed in a common grave for at least a year, with name tags. The family were not allowed the body for about one year. Jewish custom; however, was that the body receive a proper burial. Since Pilate had always shown tolerance to many of the Jewish customs and indeed, had crucified Christ due to the Jewish High Council condemning Jesus to death; Pilate willingly answered the petition of Joseph of Arimathea, who himself was part of the Jewish High Council, to bury Jesus. The tomb was not far from Golgotha and could be easily guarded by his soldiers. Furthermore, it was

---

[93] Groothius, *Apologetics,* 543

Passover and millions of people were roaming about Jerusalem which made it unlikely that anyone could steal the body unnoticed. Everyone would know where the body was laid and that would be the end of the story. Again, the women followed his body; so, they could return with spices after the Sabbath to anoint the body (Mark 15:47, Matthew 27:61).

Then Pilate decreed that the tomb be sealed by the soldiers and heavily guarded (Matthew 27: 64-66). All Roman soldiers knew very well that they faced the death penalty, were they to fail at their post or fall asleep. The apostles surely would not have wanted Jesus Christ, buried by one of the Jewish High Council since the counsel had condemned him to death. Although, scripture did say that Joseph of Arimathea was sympathetic to Jesus (Matthew 27:57, Mark 15:43, John 19:38) and had not agreed with the other members of the council (Luke 23:51). Beyond that, the apostles could not raise any objections; because, they had all scattered in fear. Peter had followed briefly; but, then in fear denied Christ. Only John was present at the cross with Mary, the mother of Jesus and Mary Magdalene; and John recorded that Joseph of Arimathea was a "secret disciple" of Christ (John 19:38).

Then, once the sabbath was over, the women returned to the tomb to anoint the body; but, the tomb was empty, and the stone was rolled away. Matthew even tells us that the soldiers had witnessed an earthquake, the stone rolled away and an angelic like being sat atop the stone; the tomb already empty (Matthew 28:1-4). The guards were very frightened and fainted; but, the chief priests paid them hush money to say the body was stolen, with a promise he would smooth things out with Pilate as well. Were the body stolen, how was it never discovered? This was the biggest case ever; and, if, the body were stolen; the Roman Army would leave no stone unturned until the body could be recovered. All they would have needed to do was find the body to disclaim the Resurrection Story. Yet, no body could be found. There were too many witnesses who knew where Jesus had been buried; so, there is no doubt the tomb lay empty.

The Transformation of Jesus Disciples

If, the followers of Christ wanted to create a reasonable, credible story to start a new religion; they were failures in telling this story. They report women as the first witnesses when women could not even speak in the court of law. Furthermore, they were a bunch of frightened apostles who at first say the women's story of seeing the empty tomb and the risen Christ, were a bunch of "idle tales" (Luke 24: 11). Certainly, if one was creating a fable, they would have not made themselves look like a bunch of bumbling fools. Knowing the ideology of those whom they would preach this new faith too; they would have had a miraculous ascension of some kind, not a body who could eat, drink, or be touched by them. This was not a religion that could be peddled to anyone; much less, by a bunch of frightened, confused men who didn't even understand when Jesus foretold this truth that he would die, be buried, and rise again. This pretty much debunks the "conspiracy theory." Surely, they could have come up with a better story and they would not have started their little religious sect in the very place all of this took place, Jerusalem.

The truth is these men transformed from frightened, mealy mouthed men to bold proclaimers of the gospel of Jesus Christ; because, they truly believed that they saw the risen Lord. Furthermore, they were teaching a religion that presented a crucified, humiliated Messiah, to Jews who only believed in a

Conquering Messiah and to Romans who thrived on honor and status. Their message would not be appealing to anyone; were it not for the Holy Spirit opening hearts to the truth. People of that time thrived on honor and status, this new gospel message would be disgusting and unwanted. Yet, they died martyrs because they truly believed they saw the resurrected Jesus.

Hallucination Theory

Already dealt with are the "swoon theory" and the "conspiracy theory." Another theory which the skeptics present is the "hallucination theory." The hallucination theory; however, also fails in its ability to produce a reasonable hypothesis; because, of several factors.

First of all, hallucinations generally occur individually and involve only one of the senses-either audio or visual. They very rarely occur as a group and when they do there is vast differences between what is experienced or accounted. Typically, hallucinations occur in a grieving period and bring a comforting message to the one grieving. Jesus; however, appeared on multiple occasions and to multiple groups, including a group of 500; which is unexplainable.

Furthermore, nothing known about hallucinations can possibly explain the conversion of Paul; who was at the top of game, powerful, a prominent leader on the rise. He hated this heretic Jesus; who, preached nonsense until he met the risen Jesus, face to face. Then, he became the chief apostle, the chief witness, and the chief apologists for the gospel. There is no way the hallucination theory could fit Paul; nor, could it fit James, the brother of Jesus.

James had thought his brother crazy, possessed, or an egotistical liar (John 7:5, Mark 3:30-35). There is no way, he would have hallucinated the risen Jesus.

After all, he did not come to the crucifixion; because, in his eyes Jesus was a small minority leader, killed shamefully who had dishonored his family name. Yet, James, the brother of Christ; became the leader of the Jerusalem church. The last place anyone would want to preach; unless, they truly saw the risen Christ.

Concluding thoughts:

Hopefully, you are beginning to get the idea of how to defend your faith in God when confronted; but, it will require study and prayer. I suggest you read *Christian Apologetics* by Douglas Groothius or *The Advancement* by L. Russ Bush. Another way to be prepared is to listen to debates or talks by Ravi Zacharias or the late Nabeel Qureshi. We can no longer sit quietly on the sidelines. It is imperative that Christians study and be always prepared to defend our faith with intellectual fervor. Then, we must teach our children to do the same.

Chapter 26

So, What Do We Do Now?

This book began as an in-depth study of the book of Nehemiah. The more I studied, the more I realized how much we, the Christians in the United States of America; needed to learn from the past. It is for that reason, I continued on with the second section of the book to help all of us to understand what has happened in our great nation.

To a great extent, we have sat by idly and allowed our faith to be questioned. All too often, we have questioned it ourselves or become too complacent to defend our faith. We have believed that there is nothing we can do. But God's grace is bigger than all our own frailties. So, what do we do now? How do we stand strong; while, at the same time humbly, lovingly present the Gospel message. That is the challenge we face, and we must find a way. I do believe we can learn a lot from the study in Nehemiah.

STANDING STRONG

We must each first examine our own hearts. Just like Nehemiah, we cannot be used to heal our nation until we first bow down in prayer before God with hearts broken by our own sin. Until our hearts break for that which breaks God's heart, we are not going to be able to face the trials before us. That prayer must be one of repentance for our own complacency. Then, we must allow God to guide us; humbly into the next stage.

As Christians, we are called to be the light and salt of the world around us. That means we must live a life that displays Christ to the world. As we do that, people will ask us, "Why do you have so much joy and hope even in the face of trials?" Then, we must be prepared to answer with truth. To do that, we must set aside time every day to study. For me, that has meant to an already packed schedule; I have gone back to school at Liberty University, so I will study more diligently. You may be more disciplined than I and can study without boxing yourself in. For most of my life I have studied the Bible every day; but, this just pushes me a little harder to remain diligent.

PRAY FOR OUR NATION

Nehemiah knew that he could not do anything without prayer. In his first prayer, he acknowledged God as the great and mighty I AM, creator of the universe; almighty and sovereign. Then, he prayed a prayer of repentance for himself, his family, and the nation. After, that he prayed God's own words and promises. He ended with a humble, committed plea for God to guide him: "I pray thee, thy servant this day" (Nehemiah 1:11). He waited for God's command; then, went, regardless of the danger and sacrifice to himself.

Are you willing to do the same? Has your heart been broken by the changes in our land? Prayer is our greatest weapon of offense. Get specific and pray for our lawmakers in Congress, pray for your co-workers, pray for your family, and pray for your church. Our nation needs a revival of faith. Furthermore, we must pray for President Trump. God chose him to be our leader and he needs our prayer. The media attacks him with all-out war. I learned during the campaign that they take his words and twist them. This I found out by listening to each speech; then, what the news media said. It did not take long to realize that what they said he said, was not what he had said.

He is not always our finest shining example of Christianity; however, neither am I, if I am honest though I strive to be with all my heart and seek God's forgiveness when I fail, as I believe he does as well. He has surrounded himself with Christians to counsel him, brought prayer back into the Whitehouse, and has placed over 23 Conservative justices with more than 40 others awaiting confirmation. With so many Satanic attacks whirling against him, I firmly believe he needs our fervent prayers to stand strong. For that reason, again to force my own hand; I place a prayer verse on his twitter feed every weekday morning and mail a prayer postcard with a Bible verse written on it every day. Most likely he never sees them; however, as a post card it passes many hands along its journey and God will have the person who needs to read it, read it.

TEACH OUR CHILDREN

One of the things that infuriated Nehemiah the most when he returned was to find that the leaders and priests had married women from other nations. This was not because of the opposition from a racial standpoint; however, the women were teaching the children false ideologies and did not teach the children to speak in Hebrew. The women were the ones teaching the children. We need to be just as concerned about what our children are learning in our school systems. I don't suggest you pluck the hair from the heads of the teachers; however, be engaged. Remember Nehemiah did not pull the hair of the women; but, he did the fathers who had failed to teach and protect their children.

Just taking our children to church is not enough. We must take time to teach them the scripture and how to pray; both by example and family study time. Become engaged in what your children are learning in school. Take the time to discuss any questions that might arise; be prepared to stand firm protecting them if bullied by other classmates or teachers. Stay intently involved.

Guide your children when they start looking for colleges. If the "IVY lead schools are teaching socialist, atheistic ideology; choose a different school. If all of the Christians in this nation did that; well, the schools would financially be forced to hire more Christian professors. There are some excellent Christian Universities out there, such as Liberty University.

REACHING OUT TO THE POOR

Nehemiah dealt in many ways with the poor in the community. He denounced those who had through greed and financial abuse, oppressed the people. Furthermore, he enacted tax reform for his people; and encouraged them to feed other people from other nations as I pointed out on page 124.

Become engaged with your community, ready to sacrifice yourself, if need be to provide for those in need. We can do more to spread the gospel of Christ by reaching out to the poor and the disenfranchised. Personally, I volunteer for two jail ministries; teaching the gospel message. For you, it may be a different ministry God calls you to; but, be ready and listen to God. He will show you where he wants you to serve.

Charity often opens the door. Be kind to all you meet throughout the day, from the cashier to the workers at the drive through window. It is amazing how far a smile and a kind word can go. Remember, how Nehemiah stood up for the unknown heroes of his day. Take the time to say thank you to your police and all those who serve or have served in the armed forces.

The church, not the government, is supposed to support the poor and the needy. However, because we failed to remember that; the government has had to step in. Let us do our part, so that the church becomes more needed and wanted than the government. Be ready to give when God asks you to; providing for your extended family and the community as God blesses you. Learn to live modestly, so that you have the funds to do this.

POLITICS

Nehemiah stood for political justice, replacing the corrupt politicians with those who would stand for justice. We, too must be engaged in politics and through voting; we can replace the corrupt politicians with those who will stand for justice.

It is imperative that we learn what a candidate stands for; then, after diligent prayer vote for those candidates God leads you to vote for. Don't listen to what the media says; study and find out for yourself what is true. Listen to the actual speeches, not someone else's thoughts about what was said. Do become engaged by calling or writing your congressmen and women.

COMMERCIALLY SUPPORT OTHER CHRISTIANS

When you have a choice of stores, restaurants and businesses; try to choose those who stand on Christian principles.

LAW AND JUSTICE

Nehemiah reestablished laws and justice in his land, knowing that no nation can survive without them.

We must stand for law and justice. That means as Christians we abide by the laws as well. Don't cheat on your taxes, don't run the stop signs because no one is looking, and don't speed, just because you don't get caught. As Christians, we need to set the example. Our nation will never survive, if we don't have laws to govern our land.

IMMIGRATION REFORM

Nehemiah led the people to build the wall and set up immigration reform. What our immigration reform looks like in the age of the church is different from that under the Old Testament; however, there must be immigration policies in place which are upheld, if we are to thrive as a nation.

For the United States, we cannot base our immigration policies on people's race or religion; nor would I want to. However, we can and should base it upon their desire to assimilate to the basic principles held within our laws and their ability to add to our society as a whole.

If we are to help the poor and needy of the world, as we should; then, we must first have a strong economy of our own. We cannot help the poor by bringing them into our own country and keeping them poor through welfare systems. Yet, we must; as I stated earlier, each be willing to live modestly so as to give to the poor of the world. We can send forth missionaries, build houses for them in their land, and teach them how to find a better life. This is a job the church must be doing.

BUILD THAT WALL

The wall is a symbol that we are a nation built on laws and principles to protect our people. It is not a symbol of bigotry or hate; rather, a symbol of national pride. Only when we stand strong as a nation, can we then be able to truly love everyone in the world. That is what Nehemiah knew. Reread Nehemiah 8:9-10.

Establishing borders, building the wall, setting themselves apart in registering, and worshipping God provided them the ability to be generous and help others in the world. Until they stood firm as a nation, they had not the ability to really be charitable. Not allowing the others in, protecting their own sovereignty as a nation; that they could do the greater good through strength; united, one nation under God.

Concluding Thoughts

We must learn from history how to move forward in this modern age. As Christians, we must be willing to take a stand to rebuild our nation; not through violence; but, through prayer, diligent study, and a willingness to obey God, whatever the personal cost. We must with humility and grace, reach out our hand in love; but, never ever compromise the truth. Learn how to defend the truth of the gospel message with intellectual rigor and never forget to teach our children.

Effie Darlene Barba

Bibliography

Allen, Leslie C. and Timothy S. Laniak. *Ezra, Nehemiah, Esther*. Grand Rapids, MI: Baker Books, 1995.

Augustine. *Enchiridion on Faith, Hope, and Love*. Translated by J.F. Shaw. Chicago: Henry Reguery, 1961.

Barba, Effie Darlene. *Abiding Steadfast Joy*. Columbia, MO: Effie de Barba Publishing, 2017.

Bautch, Richard J. *Glory and Power, Ritual and Relationship*. New York: T&T Clark, 2009.

Benthall, Jonathan. *Returning to Religion: Whay a Secular Age is Haunted by Faith*. London: Tauris, 2008.

Berlinski, David. *The Devil's Delusion*. New York: Basic Books, 2009.

Buechner, Frederick. *Wishful Thinking: A Theological ABC*. New York: Harper & Row, 1973.

Craig, William Lane. "The Kurtz/Craig Debate." In *Is Goodness Without God Good Enough?* Lanham, MD: Rowman & Littlefield Publishers, 2009.

Edwards, Jonathan. "Concerning the Divine Decrees." In *The Works of Jonathan Edwards*. Edinburgh: Banner of Truth, 1974.

Falwell, Jerry, ed. *The Liberty Annotated Study Bible.* Nashville, TN: Thomas Nelson, 1988.

Getz, Gene A. "Nehemiah." In *The Bible Knowledge Commentary: An Exposition of the Scriptures by Dallas Seminary Faculty-Old Testament,* by eds John F. Woovard and Roy B. Zuck. Colorado Springs, CO: Victor, 2004.

Groothius, Douglas. *Christian Apologetics.* Downers Grove, IL: InterVarsity Press, 2011.

Hitchens, Christopher. *God is Not Great.* New York: Hachette Books, 2009.

Josephus. "The Antiquities of the Jews." In *Josephus: The Complete Works,* by trans. William whiston. Nashville, TN: Thomas Nelson, 1998.

Klingbeil, Gerald A and Chantal Klingbeil. "Eyes to hear: Nehemiah 1,6 from a pragmatics and ritual theory perspective." *Biblica 91, no. 1,* 2010: 91-102.

Kurtz, Paul. *A Secular Humanist Declaration.* Amherst, NY: Prometheus Books, 1980.

Kurtz, Paul. "Is Goodness Without God Good Enough?: A Debate on Faith, Secularism, and Ethic." *The Kurtz/Craig Debate: Is Goodness without God Good Enough?* Lanham, MD: Rowman & Littlefield Publishers, 2009.

Kurtz, Paul. "Moral Faith and Ethical Skepticism Reconsidered." *The Journal of Value Inquiry* 19 (January 1 1985).

Kurtz, Paul. *Multi-secularism: A New Agenda.* New Brunswick, NJ: Transaction, 2010.

Kurtz, Paul. "The Promise of Manifest 2000." *Free Inquiry*, no. 5 (Winter 1999).

Lewis, C. S. *Letters to Malcom Chiefly on Prayer: Reflections on the Intimate Dialogue Between Man and God.* Orlando, FL: Harcourt, 1964.

Lewis, C.S. *Mere Christianity.* New York: HarperCollins, 1952.

MacLaren, Alexander. *MacLaren Expositions of Holy Scripture: A Reformer's Schooling.* Dallas, TX: Graceworks Multimedia, 2013.

Martin, John A. "Ezra." In *The Bible Knowledge Commentary: An Exposition of the Scriptures by Dallas Seminary Faculty: Old Testament,* by eds. John Walvoord and Roy Zuck, 651-672. Colorado Springs, CO: Victor, 2004.

McGee, J. Vernon. *Through the Bible with J. Vernon McGee: Volume II Joshua-Psalms.* Nashville, TN: Thomas Nelson, 1982.

Mill, John Stuart and Roger Crisp. *Utilitarianism.* Oxford: Oxford University Press, 1998.

Norman, Richard. *On Humanism.* 2nd. London: Taylor and Francis, 2012.

Piper, John. *Future Grace.* New York: Multnomah Books, 1995.

Rasell, Marc. *Nehemiah The Sabbath Reformer.* Kindle, 2012.

Sartre, Jean Paul. *Existentialism is a Humanism.* Translated by Carol Macomber. New Haven and London: Yales University Press, 2007.

Swift, Charles Henry. "Prayer a Vitalizing Force: The Lesson in Today's Life." *The Christian Century, no. 44,* November 1, 1917: 16.

Swindoll, Chuck. *Hand Me Another Brick, Revised ed.* Nashville, TN: Thomas Nelson, 1998.

Velarde. "Is the Bible Reliable." *Focusonthefamily.com.* n.d. https://www.focusonthefamily.com/faith/the-study-of-god/how-do-we-know-the-bible-is-true/is-the-bible-reliable (accessed January 8, 2018).

"Why Was It Important to Rebuild the Walls of Jerusalem?" *Got Questions Ministries.* n.d. https://www.gotquestions.org/rebuild-walls-Jerusalem.html. (accessed November 6, 2017).

Zacharias, Ravi. *The End of Reason.* Grand Rapids, MI: Zondervan, 2008.

www.ingramcontent.com/pod-product-compliance
Lightning Source LLC
Chambersburg PA
CBHW060835280326
41934CB00007B/791